D1553214

*Decades of Blessings*

# Decades of Blessings

### A Memoir

*Joanne*

## Joanne Gillen Cortese

RESOURCE *Publications* · Eugene, Oregon

DECADES OF BLESSINGS
A Memoir

Copyright © 2021 Joanne Gillen Cortese. All rights reserved.
Except for brief quotations in critical publications or reviews, no
part of this book may be reproduced in any manner without prior
written permission from the publisher. Write: Permissions, Wipf
and Stock Publishers, 199 W. 8th Ave., Suite 3, Eugene, OR 97401.

Resource Publications
An Imprint of Wipf and Stock Publishers
199 W. 8th Ave., Suite 3
Eugene, OR 97401

www.wipfandstock.com

PAPERBACK ISBN: 978-1-6667-3037-1
HARDCOVER ISBN: 978-1-6667-2179-9
EBOOK ISBN: 978-1-6667-2180-5

SEPTEMBER 22, 2021

# Contents

# Dedication

*D*ecades of Blessings grew from just that: years and years of blessed experiences and especially the interactions/ friendships with good, generous and inspiring people who have graced the lives of Jim and Joanne Cortese and the Gillen and Cortese extended families. Over and over, Jim and I say, "Such good people," when we think about YOU. If you are reading this, you are undoubtedly one of those "good people."

Jim and I, our children, and extended families all grew up and prospered on the shoulders of special people who loved God, their families, communities, country, and the land. As parents, teachers and mentors, Jim and I have tried to emulate that message to others. This writing is another attempt to encourage those descendants who follow us to cherish their own heritage.

We love and appreciate our own special blessings:
Brian and Becky Sorenson Cortese
Nate and Ella Cortese
Jackie Cortese and Marty Mrachek
Mason and Sienna Mrachek.

# *Preface*

This communication started when Adrian Gillen and Lisa Barta visited the Gillen Family Home, three miles south of Faribault, Minnesota in March 2021. Lisa took photos. When she left her Dad, age 92, at his home in Faribault, she suggested to him that he write his memories. Later that day, he hand-wrote two pages of memories. Later, he added more pages which are incorporated here.

I typed them, added ideas, shared them with Adrian and Lisa, and told them I would record other memories. This led to my recording my own memories. At eighty-six years of age and having been encouraged frequently by my husband Jim Cortese to write my life story, Part 2 happened! Suddenly, I realized I was writing my life story without planning to do so.

My audience is primarily our four grandchildren, providing them the opportunity to learn more about their grandparents and the heritage that is their own. They are active, smart teen-agers now, always with multiple and varied activities. In many ways, their lives and their future seem so different than mine were at their age. On the other hand, their hopes and dreams for the future probably are similar to mine when I was a teen-ager in the 1950s. We are all gifted by God and blessed with abundant self-confidence.

# Part 1

## *The Gillen family home, family farm, its homemakers, and workers*

D ad Sebastian bought what became the Gillen home in 1920. He and Cecilia, his wife, wanted their kids to go to Catholic school in Faribault about three miles from the farm. John, Ambrose, Greg, and Rita started elementary education at St. Lawrence School in Faribault after that move. The rest of us followed, 1921 to 1952.

I think of 1920 as the year of passage of the Nineteenth Amendment to the U.S. Constitution that allowed women to vote, especially our mother and the right that was now hers. In 1920, Mom was 29 years old, had a husband and four living children, had lost a baby, cared for her husband, her home, and probably some farm chores along with Church activities and doing good wherever she could. Power-playing men far away made the decision that women like her could finally vote.

In 1925, John became the driver of a horse and buggy in fair weather and a "cutter" sleigh in snowy weather. Rita was in first grade and the four siblings went to St. Lawrence School in Faribault together in the buggy. Those four children only spoke German. As they learned English, so did their parents and siblings. Dad had made arrangements with the O'Brien Ice House, about one mile from school, to board the horse and buggy during the school day in exchange for hay. Sometimes the Friesen boys, Al and Leo, rode with them. John the driver left the horse and ran to school. He repeated the process at the end of the school day.

On their way home from school one day, they encountered a problem. A farm was situated where the Rice County Fairgrounds is now. Kids from that farm threw rocks at the horse. The horse charged through its harness and ran home. The kids, of course, were left sitting safely and scared in the buggy.

Luella started school in 1927. At that time, the family owned a horse named Duke. Duke was given the proud task of taking the three siblings to and from school. Greg was now the driver. Occasionally, a neighbor Mabel Friesen rode with the Gillen kids. After school one day in the spring, Greg went to get the horse and someone else had taken Duke's bridle which included blinders. Greg used the bridle that was left. Duke had always worn blinders and as soon as cars were encountered, Duke spooked, jumped, fell, and was fatally injured.

When Mabel was late, her dad drove their car to the school, picked up the kids, and drove Central Avenue only to encounter a scared and dejected Greg walking toward the school. The whole family was saddened by the experience.

The next transportation-to-school step was provided by neighbor Jake Friesen who took his milk to a dairy in town daily. Jake removed the back seat of his vehicle, put in the milk cans, covered them with a blanket, and the Gillen kids and his granddaughter were the riders, wherever they fit in the vehicle. The kids usually walked home from school, wishing a buggy was still available. Fortunately, worry about kidnappers or adult abusers was never a reality and never even considered a threat.

These horse tales leads to a story Ambrose told about our Dad, Sebastian. When Sebastian was a young teen-ager, a neighbor asked his parents if Sebastian could go to Northfield to pick up a midwife when his wife went into labor, likely on short notice. Sebastian had driven the buggy on country roads and he did know how to get the eight or so miles to Northfield, but he didn't know Northfield streets or localities. Sebastian was told that when he got to Northfield to hold the reins loosely as "the horse knows the way." Sebastian followed directions. Presently, the horse stopped in front of a house and "Granny" came out with her bag. The two of them proceeded home in time for the baby to be delivered by Granny.

Luella, Ann, Ed, Joe, Adrian and Joanne were born in the Gillen Family home. The Gillen house, now a reddish color, was painted white until after the property was sold in the 1980s.

The three big trees south of the house stand tall and elegant like they plan to stand for another hundred years. The portion of house farthest to the west is the winter porch (year round); the room behind it was a new room, the parlor, both built in 1932, along with a full basement which included a small room where the beehives and bees were stored in the winter. The rest of the basement had a furnace and wood was used to heat the whole house.

Two other trees near the road were planted from seedlings by Ann and Adrian during the 1940s. They've grown to be huge trees. There's also an evergreen seedling that Dad planted. We always called it the "little evergreen." Of course, it too is tall and stately. At one time, the front yard had at least two apple trees and other apple trees west of the house.

In 1947 December the 8th, the house caught fire in the corn cobs in the original basement. (Dry corn cobs were used to start fires.) Much smoke damage was done as no water from the pump house was piped to the house. That winter was spent remodeling. An upstairs room was vented to install a bathroom. The following summer, water from the pump house was pumped to the house to add running water to the house. The trench was dug by hand and it still operates today.

The kitchen was changed about 1937. The old kitchen was moved away from the house and became a place to start baby chicks and later, was converted to a shop. It still stands. The woodshed north of the house was used for split firewood that was burned in the kitchen stove. Mom cooked on a wood stove her entire life. She did have a two-burner, portable electric stove as a secondary cooking source. Next to the woodshed was a smaller building that was used for smoking meat. Each winter or early spring, beef or hogs were butchered and some of that meat was hung to cure and was smoked in the smoke house.

As part of the federal New Deal legislation in 1938, REA (Rural Electric Access) became a reality for many farmers, including neighbors as near as the Friesen farm northwest of us. However, REA would not cross the railroad tracks which were about ½ mile northwest of the farm. For a few years, the Squires' farm southeast of us had electricity from Northern States Energy. When Dad fussed about it, Northern States Energy refused to extend the line to the Gillen farm as Northern States Energy said power used would not cover their cost to extend the power lines to the Gillen farm.

In 1942, however, electricity was installed: 40 kilowatts a month for $4.00. At that time, the only light bulb was in the kitchen. If it was near the end of the month and the current bill was less than $4, the light was burned so the Gillens got their money's worth. A short time later, Dad bought milking machines. That used the monthly $4. expenditure without burning the kitchen light for extra hours.

Sometime after that, Dad bought a television: 8x8, black and white, with two channels. At threshing time, a crew moved from farm to farm to thresh. Mom always made a full meal at noon for all the threshers, 12 or more men, and served in the dining room. Not many people had a TV and the threshers would watch TV during their meal. I doubt that they ate any less meat, potatoes, homemade bread, pie that Mom prepared so well. Imagine preparing two meals a day for twelve or more men. Mom wasn't "employed" of course!

Mom probably wanted a refrigerator when Dad bought the TV. The refrigerator followed soon.

Threshing of small grains (wheat, barley, oats) separates the valuable seeds from the chaff which are stems and leaves used as straw bedding for farm animals. Walt Graham, a local farmer, owned a threshing machine. Walt and others, Pa; Joe Meillier; Jake and Leo Friesen; Matt, Hank and Mike Kotz formed a threshing ring. Walt moved his machine from one farm to the next and all workers helped thresh where the machine was located. Walt owned an F20 Farmall tractor that furnished power to run the machine to separate seeds and chaff.

Leo Friesen heckled Walt repeatedly that the F20 Farmall didn't have enough power to operate the threshing machine to maximum efficiency. Leo's teasing probably incited stimulating conversation among the threshers.

One day while farming at the Gillen place, a truck drove in with a new Allis-Chalmers tractor on the truck. The truckers unloaded the tractor, attached it to the threshing machine in place of the F20 Farmall. The workers were in awe and could scarcely believe the miracle before their eyes.

Pa started conversing with the Naumans (tractor dealership) about the F20, as Walt had traded it for the Allis-Chalmers. And, certainly to the surprise of the Gillen boys, Pa bought the F20 for $400. Later, Walt told dad that he had a cultivator that mounted on the tractor and told Pa to come and get it.

Cultivating at that time was done by the Gillen boys, Ed, Joe and Adrian. They each drove a team attached to a single row cultivator. That kept them busy and out of trouble for weeks each summer. Eventually, they were replaced by a tractor and cultivator.

Threshing continued several more years until Pa bought a new combine which cut the standing grain and separated the seeds from the chaff. It decreased physical labor considerably.

During World War II, new farm equipment was not being produced as those factories were dedicated to producing equipment needed for the War. A farm auction was being publicized which included an M Farmall tractor for sale. Pa told the boys, "We are going." Word spread that several farmers were interested in the M Farmall tractor.

As the sale opened, the auctioneer announced that the M Farmall tractor had been priced by the U.S. Government at $1200. Any farmer present who wanted to bid and had the $1200 cash was asked to put their name in a hat and the name drawn could purchase the tractor. Sebastian Gillen's name was drawn! Imagine that excitement!

With apprehension and joy, Adrian drove the tractor home. This bigger tractor shortened the time needed for field work. So, Pa rented additional acreage, including Walt Graham's farm.

Another 1946 equipment story that still thrills my brother was the purchase of a four-row corn planter. It was listed for sale at an auction. Pa and Adrian went to the auction. Pa thought the bidding went too high. On the way home, father and son stopped at Priebe Implement in Waseca and bought a new four-row corn planter. Both were proud and happy, and again, less time and physical labor was needed. My brothers were getting older and more independent. Dad was likely planning for his and their futures, fewer workers and more acreage.

Filling silo was also a neighborly task. Corn was cut and elevated into the top of the silo where it would ferment and soften. Silage would be removed at the base of the silo and fed to cows. The nearest neighbors, Friesens and Meilliers, and the Gillens had silos. Together, they purchase a silage cutter. Jake Friesen kept the knives sharp and the machine was stored in his shed. The Gillens and the Meilliers furnished the power, as the Friesens did not have a tractor.

It was hard work. The corn was cut with a binder. The bundles were picked up with horses and a wagon and hauled to the cutter near the silo. On a good day, enough corn bundles could be hauled to fill a silo in that day. As time went on and machinery advanced, a corn chopper pulled by a tractor cut the corn, blew it into a wagon, and then blown into the silo with a conveyor. I doubt that anyone missed the hard work of the binder, bundles, and cutter days.

Corn picking too changed. Some corn was prepared as silage. Some corn was shredded. Bundles dried in the field were hauled to a shredder near the farm buildings. The dry leaves and stalks were shredded and blown into the barn and the ear corn was put into a corn crib with slatted sides to assure continued drying of the corn. Pa and Joe often teamed up to use the shredder for other farmers.

Adrian remembers with joy and some melancholy farming in the 1960s and 1970s farming his own land and Pa, now aged into his late Seventies, helped him often. Pa loved to work the land for planting and was always eager to see the results at harvest time. In the fall after the corn was picked, Pa was equally eager to plow. I remember Clem Gillen saying the same things about his father, Ambrose, at a similar age. That spring eagerness and fall tiredness is an experience felt by most farmers even today.

Back to the farm home. . . the kitchen always had a hardwood floor, not easy to keep clean. Luella had been badgering Dad about putting linoleum on the kitchen floor. One day, he laid a $100 bill on the floor and said, "Do you think this would work for a new floor?" Linoleum followed.

And a few more childhood memories. . . Adrian remembers his fourth grade teacher with affection. He and a couple friends liked to eat lunch quickly and wander east to the caves along the Cannon River. Some of those caves were used to brew Fleck's beer; others were used to age Treasure Cave blue cheese which had a national reputation. Others were caves, perfect for exploration by ten-year-old boys.

On one exploratory day, the boys got lost and couldn't readily find their way out. When they did find an exit, it opened unto a meadow, totally unfamiliar to the explorers. As flowers were readily available, each boy picked flowers while figuring how to get back to school. They knew they were late and flowers may be their ticket to the afternoon in school.

It worked! Sister accepted the flowers gifts, asked no questions, and they told no lies. What a beautiful memory of an understanding teacher, so special it is remembered eighty-plus years later!

Adrian remembers Martin Kleinsorg, the janitor at St. Lawrence Parish, very well. Every day, Martin cleaned the whole school carefully. His wife Victoria rang the church bell at noon daily, as a reminder to pray the Angelus prayer. One day when Adrian was in sixth grade and Ed in eighth grade, Martin asked the boys to help him dig a grave. Martin rode his bike to the St. Lawrence cemetery north of Faribault. Adrian and Ed met him there on their way home from school. That's when Adrian's six-decade grave-digging career started.

Adrian dug a grave alone at age eighteen for a man named Leo Hansen. His daughter was in Adrian's class in school. Digging the grave, Adrian reflected about the fact that Leo was quite young, a realization that not all people do grow old. In recent years at St. Lawrence Cemetery, Adrian sometimes visited that grave and the graves of many other particularly special people. Good people all. Many are still remembered by a faithful grave-digger.

Another school story features Joe. Before school one day, Joe ripped his pants – bad, as no crotch was left in place. He ran home, changed his pants, and ran back, all in record time! Adrian remembers another Joe story, which could have been a tragedy. A piece of machinery cut Joe's upper lip so badly that it had to be wired shut for six weeks. Fortunately, it healed and even his teeth were in place when the stitches were removed.

It is clear that the Gillens loved the land and all the blessings that came to them individually, as well as to the family, and to the ten families that continue the story. Good people, all.

# Part 2

## *Joanne's Life Story*

My childhood differed from my siblings. Sometimes I felt like an only child! John and Florence were married the same month I was born. Ambrose and Ruth married when I was three years old. For several years before Greg married when I was five years old, I followed him around the farm as he did his daily tasks, as the other kids were in school. When Varian entered his life, she also entered mine, and I loved her from the beginning of their relationship. When Greg bought a Model T car, I was often invited on their "dates," a five-year old chaperone I guess.

As teen-agers, Joe and Ed became interested in girls. They even confided in me about some of their feminine interests. I remember one Sunday when Mom and Dad planned a day trip to New Market which meant all of us kids were expected to participate. Joe had made other plans, and he grumbled, "If only a guy didn't have relatives!" A trip to New Market meant an afternoon with one of Mom's siblings and that person's family. Our family visited relatives often on Sunday afternoons, or that relative's family came to our home as "company."

Rita and Lue worked for families in Faribault from an early age. In the 1940s, Rita and Lue worked in Minneapolis as employment for women became available in places where men had worked prior to going into the military. Some factories converted machinery to produce items needed for war. Rita and Luella lived with two or three other young women who were employed similarly.

Ann was home to help Mom, so she and I spent time together daily. I started baking at an early age under her guidance. After her marriage to Alexius Thissen in 1946, I enjoyed their whirlwind courtship. As their November date came closer, I participated in the planning for the wedding, including killing and preparing chickens for the wedding dinner in our home. At the same time, I began to realize that Ann would move into her own home and would no longer live with us which made me very sad. Of course, I thought I was the only family member who felt that way; in retrospect, I know that wasn't true.

Ed's and Joe's courtships and marriages were the next family event. As sons, the marriage events were largely in the hands of the brides' families i.e., the Haug and the Simmons' families. Of course, both weddings were lovely and meaningful. Joe and Lorraine moved East after their marriage in Faribault, so the sadness I experienced when Ann left became a reality again, probably even more intense as they moved farther than Clara City, Minnesota. Ed and Barb lived with us for a few months after their marriage in January 1949. On Valentine's Day that year, they gave me a box of candy and I was overwhelmed with gratitude for their love and care for me.

When I was in high school at Bethlehem Academy, Adrian and I were best buds. He could drive, so when I had events at school or wanted to spend time with high school friends, he made sure I could attend. I did help him with milking chores and the housework was my responsibility.

Rita and Luella attended BA for one year each. My parents encouraged education, but my siblings had work readily available and may have felt somewhat compelled to help at home or to become employed. Much later in life, several siblings pursued and received a GED.

Robert Gillen, John and Florence's oldest son, was born less than a year after me. Dick, their second son, was born just after my third birthday, and Janet and Jeanne soon after. So, they were like siblings to me and I loved spending time with them. They spent time with us too, the boys more than Janet and Jeanne. When the boys and I were pre-schoolers, a gravel pit was being dug on John's farm. We loved playing in that gravel. One day when the workers were having lunch, Dick and I played in one of the pits being dug, sliding down and trying to crawl back up. Suddenly, we realized that the digging would resume soon. Actually crawling to solid ground was very difficult as we would continually slide back down. We did make it to the top before work resumed. We probably didn't tell anyone, as we were scared and didn't want any further reprimands or punishment.

I was just enough older than they were that I learned to read before they did. They had books and I loved to read. Their family had a big leather chair with wide wood arms. Each boy would sit on the arms and we three girls could fit side-by-side. I loved it and apparently, they did too, as we all stayed in the chair for hours at a time. One evening, relatives of Florence visited and the guests included a girl about my age. She was dressed to the nines and during the evening, she was invited to sing for the adults. The kids and I were in a bedroom reading. Later, Florence commented to us that this relative had such a beautiful voice etc. Janet and Jeanne spoke up immediately, "Yes, Mom, but Joanne knows how to read." It still makes me proud.

Robert, the oldest son, died two days after a diagnosis of bulbar polio in 1948, the first death in the Sebastian Gillen family. Dick, Janet and Jeanne also experienced polio shortly after Bob's death. Dick was in a body cast for months. Each of them experienced post-polio pain in later life. Bob's death was a significant loss for me, as he was my close friend. All family members, both immediate and extended families, faced his death-too-soon with great sorrow and grief.

I remember the childhoods of Ambrose and Ruth's children, especially Rosie and Clem. I remember Jake Gillen, Greg and Varian's oldest son standing in his crib looking out the window and I was certain that his first word was "cow." The summers when I was eight or older, I would always spend time with each of those families. I knew how to do dishes and similar tasks. I would spend time in the house and in the yard with the kids. Several years ago, Peter Gillen and I were visiting about his childhood and when I mentioned those summer visits, he said, "OH, you were the baby-sitter." I guess I was, but at that time a title was not needed. I received gifts sometimes, but it definitely was not a paid position. Varian made sure I had my own room. By the time, that room was needed for their expanding family, I was too busy to be a summer baby sitter.

Greg, Ed, and Adrian's families remember Sunday mornings after Mass and visiting at our family home. Each week without complaint, Mom prepared two dinners. Typically, she fixed goulash (ground beef, pasta, and tomato sauce) for the kids who had their meal first. The adult meal was then served. Usually that menu included meat, potatoes, vegetables and dessert. On holidays or special occasions, the adults were served in the dining room and the kids in the kitchen. I was still a kid, so I ate with my nieces and nephews. When Greg's and Ed's families became too large, they went to their own homes after Mass on Sundays. Adrian's family continued that custom until the 1960s. Gillens have always loved to gather. Several years after Mom's death, some of her grandchildren started a custom of annual family reunions which still continue on alternate years. Typically, 200-300 family members celebrate together at these festive occasions.

Rita, Luella, Ann and Ed's children came along and the familiar pattern for me continued in those families also. Rita was ill with post-partum depression after Kathleen's birth and I was with the Franke's for quite some time when Kathleen and later Bill, were babies. I helped Lue and Ann with canning and gardening, and of course, with kids! Rita's twins were born when I was a Sister. I didn't get home every summer then, but I did get to know them later in their lives. When they were ten and I lived in Anaconda, Montana, Rita, Mom, Dad, Ron and Don took the train to Montana and stayed with us at the convent for several days. It was a great time and it was a memorable trip for them. On the train, the huge boulders east of Butte are right at train-window level, and Mom remembered "those rocks" for ever after. (Helen and Don Martin also visited me in Anaconda. Later, Lisa and Steve Barta visited me and my family in Butte. Both couples were on their honeymoons, and I was told that my Dad strongly suggested that they visit me on their respective wedding trips. Helen and Don, of course, had the privilege of being convent guests each in a room with a single bed, very likely the only time that happened either before or after 1968.) I have never known another Sister who entertained honeymooners in the convent.

Joe and family moved to Wisconsin on a farm he bought when I was a teen-ager. David, their oldest son, was born in 1950 and I left home in 1952, so I didn't know Joe's children as children and I have always felt that loss. By the time Adrian's children were school-age, Jim and I had children of our own. We visited my parents every summer at least and almost always stayed with Adrian, Jeanne and their family. Our kids loved and respected those cousins and have continued to appreciate them all their lives.

We stayed with Ed the summer visit after Barb died. Jackie loved going to the kitchen window in the morning and checking out the farmyard. She said, "I love the smell of manure. It's a natural high!" Neither I nor my siblings had ever entertained that thought!

My high school experience at BA was a good one, definitely a growth experience in so many ways. I had good teachers, did well in my classes, and I made new friends. I was responsible for Prom decorations in 1950, and I had the lead in the school play the same year. Ironically, the play was called *Murder in A Nunnery*. Of course, I wore a likeness of a Dominican habit. One year, I wrote a weekly column in the *Faribault Daily News* about school activities or teen-age concerns. I was paid $1.00 an inch! It was my first paid job! I was third academically in my class of 1952. In the 1970s when I came home, several BA. classmates and I had lunch or breakfast together each time I came. Until Covid in 2020, we still did get together. If the opportunity presents itself again, we all would like to continue the practice. About half of the Class of 1952 has died, including several of the group mentioned here

Spring of my Senior year, I decided, with some hesitancy, that I would enter the Congregation of the Dominican Sisters of Sinsinawa, Wisconsin to pursue life as a Catholic Sister. Dominicans had been my teachers for twelve years and I was impressed with them and their lives. Four girls from the previous class at BA had entered the Dominicans including my good friend, Marian DeGrood. Three other girls from my own class entered with me, although I was not aware of that until September when I met them at the Mound, the name the Sisters used for their Sinsinawa Motherhouse.

Sisters were not an anomaly in our family. Dad Sebastian had two sisters in the Benedictine Congregation in St. Joseph, Minnesota. Our first cousin, Anne Marie Reuvers, joined that group in 1947. Grandma Susan Wagner had two sisters who were Benedictine Sisters in Duluth, Minnesota. Grandma Wagner spent the final years of her life with them in their Care facility in Duluth and Grandma died there. Ursula Wagner, daughter of Mom's brother Tony and his wife Antoinette and several of her sisters, as well as a daughter of Mom's brother Ed and his wife Evelyn, joined the School Sisters of Notre Dame in Mankato, Minnesota later in the 1950s and early 1960s. Aunts Antoinette and Evelyn Wagner had sisters in that Congregation.

I'd had good high school friends, went to Proms, and dated a few other times. I particularly enjoyed the company of Clayton LaCroix and his sisters in our neighborhood. It was a tough good-bye to family and friends. I would be home for a week the following March and then four *years* later for a week. It was definitely a commitment and I envisioned it as a commitment for life.

In retrospect, my hopes and dreams my Senior year of high school were not clearly defined. I probably would have worked at home and/or on the farm and eventually married a farmer. We didn't have career/college counselors and no one in my family had gone to college, so college or a career didn't seem possible. I do remember my sister Rita saying, "Why don't you go to St. Catherine's College in St. Paul and major in journalism?" I thought she was teasing me, and maybe she was, but I couldn't imagine how I could do that. I didn't ask many questions at that time. My parents and my siblings as well were always engaged in service to others as opportunities presented themselves. I still can "hear" Mom's voice on the telephone, "This is Mrs. Sebastian Gillen. I'm calling on behalf of St. Lawrence Parish to ask you to help . . . " The concept of *service* was very clear in my youthful mind.

The Dominican Motherhouse is located in southwestern Wisconsin across the Mississippi River seven miles from Dubuque, Iowa and East Dubuque, Illinois on a high hill property that overlooks the farmland of the area. Several other small towns are in the area. In 1952, it was isolated in the country. The property includes numerous buildings, both for the Sisters who lived there, farm workers, farm buildings, and for a high school girls' four-year boarding school, which probably paid most of the bills for the total community. In the 1950s and earlier and for some years later, the property had a full-working farm, including a dairy farm, chickens, other small animals, a large vegetable garden, prolific apple orchards, and several hundred acres of fields. Farm workers had a home on the property, enjoyed their prepared meals, as did a full-time priest chaplain, and one or more vehicle drivers. A nurse and a Sister pharmacist provided every day health needs for Sisters and students. Sisters went to MDs and dentists in Dubuque as needed. Health needs of the High School students also had to be arranged in consultation with their parents.

Students had their own dining room and recreation areas including a small gym and tennis courts. Laundry was provided at the large efficient laundry staffed by the Sisters, postulants and novices. Sinsinawa had and still has its own United States Post Office, with a Sister as Post Mistress.

During my initial years, 300-400 people lived there. During the summer, additional Sisters lived in the spaces occupied by the high school students during the school year and took classes or worked at the Mound in offices, the garden, the kitchen, or other needs required by hundreds of self-sufficient women.

A couple times annually, dozens of chickens were slaughtered. Strong-stomached novices helped with that operation. The Sisters enjoyed home-grown beef, pork, and chicken. Homemade bread, rolls, apple pie, cookies, and other baked foods were part of most meals. Oatmeal, and thankfully, cold cereal plus fruit and coffee were typical breakfasts. Milk from the farm dairy was pasteurized and always available at meals. Like most farm families, food was largely home-grown. Logistically, meeting the needs of a total community of over 500 people had to be a constant concern of several hard-working Sisters. A bustling business office was part of the operation and somehow by the grace of God "made ends meet."

The first years as a postulant and novice were preparation for religious life. I took college classes, did chores like helping with laundry, dishes, housekeeping. We prayed together several times a day, made visits to the Chapel, did spiritual reading, and participated in daily Mass. Much of the time was silent with an hour or two of recreation each afternoon and occasionally in the evening. Even meal times were silent. A Sister read spiritual books aloud during the noon and evening meals. Most evenings were spent studying for classes. Both an afternoon and an evening snack were the norm. In September 1952, fifty to sixty women entered the Congregation with me from all over the country; many from Chicago, other parts of Illinois and the Midwest, one from each New York, Nebraska, and Arizona. Most were high school graduates like me; some had some college or employment experience. The oldest, in her thirties, one Black woman who graduated from the Dominican high school in Mobile, Alabama, and dozens of white teen-agers made up this diverse group of postulants. Most became good friends. In August 1954, forty-three of us were professed for three years as Dominicans. We had worn the Dominican habit for one year as a novice, along with a white veil; at that ceremony, I became named Sister Adrienne. At profession, we each began to wear black veils with the white habit. Most of the crowd became teachers that September. Immediately after profession, we all spent a week with seasoned teachers in a school setting in East Dubuque, Illinois. Then, most of my crowd were off to a classroom of their own in various parts of the country; the average age was likely twenty years. In most cases, at least one seasoned Sister/teacher went out of her way to assist this fledgling teacher with little preparatory education and no teaching experience. When traveling to those sites, each carried a small bag, had a train ticket, and much apprehension. Each had a trunk with all her possessions which was typically trucked to the convent (new residence) of the owner.

With three others from my crowd, my third year was spent at Edgewood College in Madison, Wisconsin as a full-time college student. Again, we had household duties, slept in a dormitory with curtains between beds, and occupied by fifteen or more women in a home for about forty Sisters. Teachers were Dominicans who were full-time college professors, as was the college President, Dean of Students, and financial officials. Other teachers were professors from the University of Wisconsin at Madison. We interacted with some of the regular college students; one good friend became a Dominican after her college graduation. We continued to be good friends until her death last year. In the 1950s, Edgewood was a women's college. The campus included a four-year co-ed High School and a K-8 elementary school. Edgewood's main focus at that time was teacher preparation, so most college students spent time at the Campus School or Edgewood High School, observing and serving as teacher aides.

The Sisters lived together in the original building on campus. We had daily Mass in the chapel, said the Divine Office morning and evening, along with other prayers and the rosary. We had our own dining room and had household responsibilities, studies, and more personal time than the previous two years.

The Franke family visited me there once. Bill was in Kindergarten and he liked to sing "On top of Old Smoky" and similar songs. Many Sisters asked him to sing and he got tired and as grumpy as one would expect of a five-year old. High school friends, Carole Shields and her fiancé Dale Andersen visited also at another time. It was brave of them to visit me in such a different environment than the familiar events of high school social events. It forced me to renew my commitment to a celibate life as a Dominican Sister.

In August 1955, I was assigned to teach second grade at Epiphany School in southwest Chicago (25th Street and Keeler Avenue). I lived in a convent next to the school with twelve other Sisters. One Sister served as the cook; the others were teachers. We had daily Mass in our Chapel or the parish Church, said the Divine Office morning and evening, along with other prayers and the rosary. People like me needed many preparatory hours each evening in anticipation of the school day ahead.

Fifty-seven students made up my first class with about 600 kids in Epiphany school, fairly typical numbers in large city schools in the 1950s. Each child had a desk, but there was very little aisle space. The school had no gym or gathering space and no playground. Other Sisters helped me a bit with lesson plans/suggestions. Essentially, I was on my own! As the first day was ending, a boy vomited in front of me. No janitor was available, so clean-up was also teacher responsibility. I survived, and continued teaching second grade for three more years, then taught a combination of third and fourth graders, some of the same kids I'd taught in second grade. I improved at teaching. I don't remember feeling totally confident with all the responsibilities; I was always learning. Occasionally, I still hear from several people in those early classes. Three girls from those years and that parish joined the Dominicans and now are retired Sisters.

As second grade teacher for four years, I prepared those children for reception of both Sacraments of Penance and Holy Eucharist each spring. Children received Holy Communion as a group at a Sunday Mass. Parents dressed their children elaborately for the occasion and they were special days. Preparation was a challenge and a privilege way beyond the comprehension of seven-year olds.

Almost every Saturday all those years, those of us who didn't have a college degree went to class. Sometimes, classes were taught at Visitation High School, a Dominican School, by a credentialed and qualified Sister. Edgewood College made the arrangements and recorded the credits toward Graduation. I also took Saturday classes at Loyola and DePaul Universities and always went to summer school, usually at Edgewood College. Saturday classes always required a city bus trip, one hour each way. That was typical transportation to medical or similar appointments. Several parents offered to drive us where we needed to go, and that happened fairly often to meet the needs of thirteen adult women who were full-time teachers. The additional gift to us was long-time, valued friendships with the drivers; their friendship was reciprocated. Wonderful, generous people.

On Sundays at Epiphany, the Sisters counted the collection from the Sunday Masses which took several hours. It was never a favorite task. That was the only parish in my experience that expected the Sisters to do that task.

Weekly, the Sister who handled the convent finances and I would walk to Piggly Wiggly about six blocks with a shopping basket on wheels to buy groceries. Buying for a large household resulted in lots of groceries to lug home. We wore heavy black mantles, so the hotter it was outdoors, the hotter we were walking home! Vegetable peddlers moved around the neighborhood one day weekly. We were in school, of course, but a neighbor would check on our needs and make vegetable purchases for us.

Monsignor Cummings, our pastor, enjoyed buying sweets from a local bakery and he often left doughnuts and other goodies in our kitchen. He had a gruff exterior, but he was kind-hearted. He hated it when kids left an outside school door open, especially when the weather was cold. One day, first graders were outside and he followed them into school. Sure enough, the door was left open. He walked right into the classroom and yelled, "Who in here was born in a barn?" A child raised his hand and said, "Jesus." Monsignor turned around and walked out!

Another time when I had the second graders in the church, he came in and talked to the kids for a few minutes. Some child answered his question by referring to the entrance to the church as "the back of the church". Monsignor didn't like that answer and he said, pointing to the entrance, "That's the front of the church. You come in the *front* door." Then, he asked the location of the tabernacle. (I listened closely.) A child answered pointing to the altar, "Up there.

. . in the back of the church." I think Monsignor left that time also!

One of the first days of the 1959-60 school year, newlyweds Rosie and Kenny Becker visited me. Kenny drove Rosie and me to the Museum of Science and Industry near Lake Michigan, at least an hour drive from the convent. Traveling that far in the city in late afternoon through several minority neighborhoods was an unforgettable experience for my guests. We did enjoy the time together and I felt honored that they chose to spend that special time with me and I thanked God, our adventure was safe.

In the fall of 1960, I started teaching Grades Five and Six at St. Patrick School in Bloomington, Illinois, and lived with three other Sisters. It was an old school with small classrooms. Kids' desks were side-by-side across the room. If a kid stood up, the rest of the row had to pull in their chairs, so the walking kid could get out of the row. They were nice kids and that had been their pattern in previous years. The second year in Bloomington, I taught the same kids in Grades Six and Seven. I liked the kids, most of whom had stable families. That school did have a small playground, but no gym or meeting room. The convent too was small. We did have a chapel, but no daily Mass. Other prayers were the same. Most evenings were spent preparing for classes, taking care of personal needs, and laughing a lot. We took turns with meal preparation and housekeeping. The school did have a capable janitor. Occasionally only, we watched television, primarily the election when John F. Kennedy beat Richard Nixon.

The summer of 1960, I received a BA degree in history from Edgewood College. I also had nearly enough credits to have a degree in Education as well. Although I'd been a part-time student for years, I really never thought about actually earning a Degree. I did participate in the

Graduation ceremony, as did a number of Sisters and dozens of graduates.

The next year, I taught sixth grade in Mobile, Alabama. That August, Louise Gillen was professed as a Maryknoll Sister in St. Louis, Missouri. I was there. I don't remember how I got there, but my brother Greg took me and Pete to the train depot when we were leaving St. Louis. However, he didn't plan enough time for the trip to the airport and I missed my train departure. Pete was a new Holy Cross Brother at that time and was assigned to a mission in New Orleans.

Somehow, we negotiated a trip to New Orleans for each of us. Pete and I went together to New Orleans and I went with him to the monastery where he was to be stationed. It must have been a shock to have this young Brother arrive at his new assignment in the company of a woman, a Sister, Aunt or not. I was able to take a train from New Orleans to Mobile. For us Sisters in those days, our travel tickets were purchased in advance and we didn't carry any money. Greg must have picked up the tab, as I doubt that two different train companies were happy to accommodate a switch of tickets like that! I don't remember telling other Sisters about my overnight train trip with a male companion! Personally, traveling with a nephew was not a big deal. After all, we were childhood friends.

Most Pure Heart of Mary Parish in Mobile was established to serve the Black community about 1935. Dominicans had taught there many years. Grades One to Twelve in two school buildings, a church, and a convent for sixteen Sisters made up the campus. Each classroom in the elementary school had its own entrance, as building heat was not an issue. HEAT was an issue. For most months, the temperature was at least in the 80s and the humidity 80+. Weather alone was a unique experience. The kids' stories about their home life were often shocking experiences, most of which were beyond my youthful imagination.

In retrospect, I regretted not being better prepared to live and teach in a totally different culture. Even understanding the dialect (language) was difficult. Some language phrases had unique meanings. For example, the words "carry" and "fixin." One sixth grader, Jerome, was taller than I, and probably 75 pounds heavier than I. One evening, his mother called me: "Sistah, Romie won't be in school tomorrow as I'm FIXIN to CARRY him to the Doctor." That image baffled me; I thought he must be very ill to need to be carried. When I shared the story with another Sister, she clarified the meaning of "carry" for me. "Fixin" covered multiple words. Usually, it meant "preparing," as used by Jerome's "Mama."

The Sisters were the only white people in at least twelve square city blocks, an oasis of safety, order, and cleanliness. An open trash-filled field bordered the church property, and many city blocks neighboring that field were ghetto: shacks with few if any amenities. Lives lived in that ghetto were beyond the comprehension of a young, white woman who grew up on a Minnesota farm.

Drinking fountains and restrooms in all city buildings were labeled "White" or "Colored." We visited a nearby hospital a few times. Hospitalized Blacks were cared for in dormitories: rows of beds. Cleanliness and odor didn't seem to be a concern to the employees. The only time I remember leaving the neighborhood, essentially a ghetto, was a trip to a Florida beach of white sand. I remember no details, other than it was an extremely pleasant change. The convent had a chapel, and prayers were the same as previous years. It is strange that we Sisters didn't discuss adaptation to the culture. We just did what needed to be done. Turning on a light in the kitchen after dark resulted in cockroaches crawling like crazy on a mission all their own.

Fall 1962, the U.S and Russia were at loggerheads about the political situation in Cuba and it looked like war was imminent. We lived ninety miles from Cuba, so it was a frightening time for all. We did watch television at that time. We and the country were safe. In my lifetime, I had never considered that I might live in the midst of a battlefield.

Summer 1963 I studied Education Administration at Marquette University in Milwaukee, Wisconsin. That August, I was assigned to St. Martin de Porres School in Oklahoma City as principal and fifth and sixth grade teacher. One other Sister, my good friend and classmate, Sister Catherine Thomas, taught Grades One and Two, and a lay teacher, Grades Three and Four.

Travel to Oklahoma City was unique, in that I traveled on the Rock Island Railroad and was able to board in Faribault at the Depot which is now a nice restaurant. Fifty or more miles outside of Oklahoma City, those fifteen or twenty passengers boarded a one-car-plus-engine train. It was like a trip back in time that I'd never experienced. I regretted being alone, as it would have been very funny to share the experience. Baggage was loaded on the same car, along with chickens, veggies or whatever else needed transportation to Oklahoma City.

The previous year, the St. Martin de Porres Parish Church and Grades Seven and Eight, were permanently closed. The Oklahoma Bishop ruled that St. Martin's was a segregated parish and Grades One through Six would also close spring 1964. For Sister Catherine and me, our task was to teach the kids and prepare them to attend other schools the next year. Two Catholic schools with White students and teachers were located within one mile of St. Martin's. Not all St. Martin School kids were Catholic. The kids and their families loved their school and parish. The Sisters taught there for over thirty years and were well respected in that segregated community. Essentially, it was a potentially volatile situation: much distrust, distress, and anger but thankfully, nothing exploded. Parents and students were unhappy, but they seemed to realize that Sister Catherine and I had no control over the situation. Whether or not, unhappy people contacted the Bishop remains unknown.

No other Dominican Sisters had ever integrated an all Black school into, hopefully, Catholic schools that would be racially integrated. Nor, did we receive any guidance or direction about how integration was supposed to happen. We did the best we could and were never informed of what happened after we left, probably nothing significant. It's a good memory in some ways, yet the situation was a travesty of justice. If we had had a little guidance, the situation would likely have had a more positive closure. To this day, I wonder if any of those children went to a Catholic or a public school. It was a situation with good intentions on the part of the Bishop, but little or no preparation or plan for a realistic future for the families who would continue living there.

We lived in the small convent next to the school. We were the only white people for miles around, but it was a safe neighborhood. A woman friend of the previous pastor, at his suggestion, really looked out for us. We had no transportation. She either took us to the store or purchased groceries for us. Catherine and I were friends then and continue to be friends now! I had had the year in Mobile in a somewhat similar situation. Catherine had no experience living in a Black community. For example, kids used to come to the convent and ask, "Hey, Catholics, could we use your basketball?"

Like Mobile, temperatures in Oklahoma City were warm to hot most of the year. However, Oklahoma City was considerably less humid than Mobile. Being dry however resulted in dust storms unlike any ever experienced. Our home was not insulated, and after some storms, red dust an inch thick covered the windowsills and of course, the inside of the house. In spite of dust or the ghetto, many cardinals were evident in the neighborhood in February, a lovely distraction.

Mom, Dad and Greg visited us there. They never spoke of the experience. I know they, like me, were unaccustomed and likely, uncomfortable, in a totally different environment. They probably did have some reassurance that we were safe.

When Catherine and I left in June 1964, we never heard if any of the kids actually ended up in a Catholic school, or what happened to the property or any other news. A priest at a neighboring parish was kind to us. In fact, at his suggestion, we both became honorary members of the NAACP, the National American Association of Colored People and awarded a pin identifying us as members. Again, we were likely the only Dominican Sisters to be so recognized.

In no other convent at the time did only two Sisters live alone in one place as Catherine and I did in Oklahoma City. We were too innocent to be afraid. In retrospect, it could have had a terrible outcome. I wonder why the Bishop never visited that unique situation which he had ordered. The parish was abandoned by its "Shepherd." Much good could have been achieved. Catherine and I didn't have enough life experience to assist the people in their trauma and anger. I've never figured out why two 28-year olds were given that assignment.

Summer 1964, I started a Master's Degree program at Loras College in Dubuque, Iowa. It was a six-year program and in 1969, I was awarded a Master's Degree in Education Administration. That Degree also was not something I had ever anticipated.

Several other Dominican Sisters and many Sisters of other Religious Communities were enrolled at Loras. We lived in private rooms in a dorm that housed seminarians during the regular school year. Meals were served on campus. Essentially, we went to class and studied. Campus had a swimming pool. It was definitely a safe area. We had no transportation, so we either walked on campus or off campus. The Dominicans' nursing home called St. Dominic Villa was located a few blocks from Campus and I walked there several times, as I knew a number of Sisters there.

I mentioned above that I am still in contact with people that I knew at Epiphany in the 1950s. I have not had contact with students or parents from Bloomington, Mobile or Oklahoma City. The woman who befriended us in Oklahoma City died several years ago. She and I did correspond periodically prior to her death and her daughter contacted me when she died. She was originally from Chicago. She and her husband moved to Oklahoma after they purchased a business. He died suddenly. When we knew her, she was carrying on the business, seemed lonely and truly seemed to enjoy her time with us. She was a Godsend to us in our isolation.

My next mission was St. Peter School in Anaconda, Montana where I was principal and taught Grade Eight. Dominicans had taught at St. Peter's since about 1900. The records of students in early classes were handwritten in large, hard-covered record books. Frequently, I received requests for school transcripts, since those early students were applying for Social Security and proof of age was a requirement. A school record was sufficient evidence of age.

Initially, the school included both an elementary and a high school. In 1950, a new high school was built, staffed by Dominican Sisters. A convent for those teachers was prepared. In 1960, eight Sisters and two lay teachers made up the roster and the Sisters lived at St. Peter Convent. The school was a big brick square building of three floors plus a large attic. It had a small auditorium and each classroom had a coat room attached. Desks were on runners. It was a neat old school.

I took the train, the Northern Pacific Main Streeter, two days and two nights on the train from Minneapolis to Montana. The Main Streeter stopped in Logan, Montana about sixty miles east of Butte and eighty-five miles east of Anaconda. Passengers rode a bus from Logan to the Northern Pacific Depot in Butte. The Northern Pacific had a second Chicago to Seattle train, the North Coast Limited. It was more expensive and it did stop in Butte.

As mentioned before, I had a ticket. No one told me about the bus ride from Logan to Butte. Logan is located in a deep valley near the Gallatin River. The bus crawled slowly up a steep hill outside Logan and I kept looking for St. Peter School! It was August, but an early morning stop revealed snow on the ground. Obviously, these surroundings were world's apart from either Oklahoma City or Mobile.

Two women from St. Peter's met me at the train depot in Butte and drove to Anaconda. They were pleased to tell me that Interstate 90 between Butte and Anaconda had been completed just recently. The previous curvy mountain road is still drivable, but definitely not a four-lane Interstate highway. The convent was an old brick building, comfortable, but nothing fancy. It had sixteen bedrooms, so it was spacious for eight people.

We had a chapel, a large dining room, community room, kitchen, a full basement and a fenced backyard. The alley, the school playground and the convent back yard separated the convent and the school. The Church was across the street from the school. The pastor was Father Tim Moroney, born in Ireland 65+ years earlier and lived his whole priestly life in Montana. He had a thick Irish brogue and stories about him abounded throughout the Diocese of Helena. He said Mass in the convent chapel every morning at six a.m.. He was never late, and neither were the Sisters! I had not had the experience of daily Mass in the chapel in previous assignments. Tim and I became good friends over my six years at St. Peter's.

I became especially good friends with Sister Sue Klein. We were the same age. She grew up with brothers in Peoria, Illinois. She was a hard worker and loved to have a good time. Sue and I started some interaction between the seventh and eighth grade classes. She taught Math to both classes and I taught English to both classes, which eased our preparation for classes. One year we did a multi-disciplinary production of the *Diary of Anne Frank.* The kids loved the creativity and so did we. Even today, when I hear World War II music, I think of Sue and those students.

Sue and I and others who were interested did considerable exploring in Montana. One summer we taught summer Bible school in Plains, Montana. Father Jack Hunthausen, the Bishop's brother, was the pastor. The Hunthausens were a big Anaconda family, including a sister who was a Sister of Charity. Jack clearly understood that we might need some fun. So he took off for the week and left his car and a credit card for us to use, and we stayed at his house. So, we worked hard every morning, prepared for the next day, and took off in a different direction every day. That was a really good week! Jack died a few years ago. God bless him. He and his Bishop brother Dutch lived together in an assisted living facility in Helena in their last years. Both were in their nineties when they died.

Somehow, we knew the caretaker of the City Pool in Anaconda and were given a key. The facility was closed to the public on Sunday, so some Sisters went swimming nearly every week. Occasionally, we played basketball in the Anaconda Central High School gym. We became friends with a couple of the Benedictines from St. Paul School who also liked to explore. Having the Catholic high school and another convent of Sisters nearby was a pleasant new experience for me. Most of the St. Peter's graduates went on to Anaconda Central High School. Anaconda had three parishes within a couple miles. Actually, that was similar to Faribault when I was growing up.

Anaconda was a mining town. Copper was and had been mined in Butte since 1860. Initially, all mines were underground with an arrangement of tunnels and mine shafts that resembled a city's layout of streets. Elevators carried workers to various levels where they worked. One mine was one mile deep; elevators stopped about every 100 feet. Temperatures below ground were extremely hot. Ore was brought to the surface with similar elevators, moved to railroad cars and shipped to Anaconda for smelting. Prior to smelting, earth around the ore had to be removed. Ore was heated to extremely high temperatures in huge iron cauldrons of ore, poured into trays to harden, and these anodes were shipped to Great Falls where it was often made into wire. In reality, Montana copper lighted the country as the country became electrified in the late 1800s. It was dangerous work. Seeing the tubs of hot ore was a startling, frightening sight.

In the 1950s, open pit mining began in Butte. Mining started at the surface, typically a hillside, and gradually a road wound around the area mined. Ore was loaded into huge trucks. Open pit mining creates more waste (non-metal) soil. The Anaconda Company at that time claimed open pit mining was more efficient and definitely safer than underground mining. The retrieved dirt and ore then went to machines called a concentrator to separate the waste from the ore. The smelting process continued in Anaconda, until the Company found it cheaper to ship the ore to Japan for smelting. The smelting operation in Anaconda stopped in 1980.

During the 1960s, most men in Anaconda worked with copper, either on "the hill" in Anaconda or the mines or concentrator in Butte. Labor Unions did their best to protect and benefit the workers. Labor strikes were frequent then, as well as in earlier and later years. Price of copper fluctuated as one would imagine. In this dangerous environment, many Anaconda men died young. For years, the arsenic level in the mine discharges and smoke was so intense that plants or trees did not grow within many miles of the city. Quickly, I learned a lot about copper and the ups and downs of lives that depended on it, as the families of all the students in Anaconda were affected by it. Even eighth graders thought seriously about college, as most parents didn't want their children to be miners.

The previous principal was considerably older than I was at age twenty-nine. During my first week, several boys at Anaconda Central High School were cleaning the school when I visited there. Two of them had siblings in eighth grade. SO, they went home and told their families that they had seen the new principal and made up stories that put the fear of God in their siblings. One of those students was Patricia Casey who would become my lifelong friend. Over time, I've attended numerous class reunions in Anaconda, including the class of 1969 when my first class of eighth graders proudly graduated from Anaconda Central. Much reminiscing happened at those reunions. I've always enjoyed learning what happened to those graduates after they lived independently. Actually, in various settings, I was employed with a few of them and taught some of them again after 1979 when I started teaching at Montana Tech. In fact, I remember one college Freshmen who approached me at the end of class and said quietly, "My Ma said that you were at my Baptism!"

I have often wondered why I fell in love with Anaconda from the beginning. Perhaps it was the likeness to my own being a Catholic growing up on the farm near a small town. Like our childhood, most of the students in Anaconda lived in a fairly stable environment with hard-working parents and a family life. In Anaconda, it was always clear that the Sisters were respected. Unlike either the Mobile or Oklahoma City experience, most kids were part of a family. They didn't come to school with stories about a drunk dad, or a mother's boyfriends, or not having eaten for two days, or a shooting in the neighborhood.

Most Anaconda kids went to Mass, as did their parents and siblings. Most eighth grade students had been in Catholic School since first grade. They had an understanding of faith and values, unlike my previous teaching experiences.

I never knew the families in Bloomington and I don't know why. I did know families at Epiphany in the 1950s in a Catholic and highly moral environment. Most people in the immediate neighborhood were of Polish descent. Chicago was made up of distinct neighborhoods, so much so that many adults had lived only in their immediate neighborhood.

Prior to school opening in Anaconda like schools everywhere, each teacher prepared her classroom. We had meetings of all the teachers and I prepared letters and announcements for parents. A janitor was hired and the school was always cleaned and cared for.

I had about forty eighth graders and taught all subjects. The Anaconda School District invited our eighth graders to home economics and shop classes at the local Junior High twice a week in the afternoons, so I had a break twice a week. All the kids went home for lunch. We had good teachers and very few troublesome kids. I loved it.

The parish had a religion program for children that attended public schools. They met on Sunday mornings between Masses. Anaconda Central students were the teachers. Religion teachers at the high school managed the program.

Father Jim Cortese, who had been ordained in 1962 and served the parish in Deer Lodge for three years, came to St. Peters in January 1965. The pastor was well, but other than daily Mass, he didn't embrace parish activities. Jim was largely responsible for the parish and he taught religion at Anaconda Central.

We both remember the first time we saw each other. The convent needed sheets and towels and those purchases were the parish responsibility. I told Tim our needs. Tim didn't drive, so Jim's first task was to drive to Butte with Tim and buy items that the convent needed. When they returned, I was outside the school and waved to them. Tim told Jim, "That is Sister Joanne. She is the principal."

A few months later, we Sisters were notified that we could change our clothing to a more contemporary style. Patterns for a two-piece dress and a small veil were sent to us. All the Sisters at St. Peters wanted to change. Together, we contacted parish women who could sew and we invited them to a meeting. Each Sister had a seamstress who took a pattern and the material for the dresses, and they went to work. They measured each of us that evening; none of us knew what size we were. The measuring was hysterical!

Rose Byrne was my seamstress. She had a daughter younger than I who was a Dominican and a son who was a Maryknoll priest. Maryknoll priests who were in the vicinity of another priest's family visited that family. One day when I was at Rose's for her to make adjustments to my dresses, a Maryknoll priest came to the door. Rose got so excited and she pushed me in a bedroom and closed the door! I stayed there during his short visit. We had a great laugh about the near-naked Sister hiding in the back bedroom during her visit with a male visitor.

The day that we all donned our new dresses, nylons, our old black shoes, and our small veil with hair that hadn't been exposed for years was an emotional day. We knew we had to see someone other than each other before we went to a parish Mass or to school, so we all went to the rectory to have Tim and Jim see if they could recognize us. They met the challenge and gave us sufficient courage to keep wearing our new dresses! We each had two dresses.

Shortly thereafter, Patsy Pahut, a local hairdresser, asked if she could cut our hair. As a result, we looked less shabby! Her service to us continued and we were always grateful. Good people.

The Second Vatican Council convened in Rome in 1963 and changes in the Catholic Church in general and ministry in particular were being discussed and implemented at all levels in the church and gradually in the greater society. The 60s, of course, saw major changes in race relations, politics, and values. Religious Sisters took the suggested changes of the Vatican Council seriously and diligently tried to implement those changes as appropriately as possible. The dress of Religious Sisters was the most evident of changes. At the same time, dramatic changes were occurring in prayer life, religious community, and Sisters' involvement in parish life and the greater community in which Sisters lived and worked. Challenges abounded personally and in religious community. Change was the norm.

In the mid 1960s, for example, the Dominican Motherhouse Administration threatened to close St. Peter School. It may have been a response to Sisters' needing and wanting to work in environments other than schools, in essence, a response to opportunities being opened for Sisters to become involved in religious work, other than schools. I don't know if other Dominican-staffed schools were given a closure threat. Whatever the administrative reason, Anaconda families wanted to keep Catholic schools and teaching Sisters. At St. Peters, I called a parish meeting, invited Bishop Hunthausen who attended and people were invited to express their concerns. Although small, the auditorium was packed with attendees.

Following the meeting, we compiled a notebook of testimony expressed at the meeting and other written expressions from the Anaconda community. The Bishop of the time was Archbishop Raymond Hunthausen who was a graduate of St. Peter High School. He may have responded directly to the Dominican Motherhouse. Apparently, the Anaconda response was heard, as the issue of St. Peter School closing at that time was dropped.

However, in the early 1970s, the presence of Catholic schools in Anaconda was threatened again. This time, the action came from the local church, as Catholic schools were draining the operating budgets of the three parishes in Anaconda. Jim was responsible for a money-raising campaign. Ultimately, all three elementary schools and Anaconda Central High School closed in 1973. I will return to this emotional event.

The two other elementary schools in Anaconda were staffed by Benedictine Sisters from St. Joseph, Minnesota and Sisters of Charity of Leavenworth, Kansas. The latter had many Sisters serving in Montana. Both were good schools with good teachers. The three principals worked together well and we shared resources whenever possible. St. Peter Sisters made friends with the Sisters at the other elementary schools and frequent contact with the Dominicans at Anaconda Central. Acceptance and friendship was the norm and truly appreciated.

Opportunity is a small residential community a few miles east of Anaconda and Catholic residents were considered to be members of St. Peter Parish. Opportunity had its own public school called Beaver Dam School and family activities centered around the school. Some Opportunity families expressed interest in having Sunday Mass at the school auditorium sometimes. Vatican II emphasized the importance of small communities and their request was right in line with that Catholic Church thinking. As a result, Father Cortese began to celebrate Mass in Opportunity once a month. It was well received and the people were so grateful and seemed to feel special.

With the enthusiasm of the success of that venture, I was the instigator of establishing religious education for the children from Beaver Dam School. Five or six non-employed mothers were recruited and each had a group of five or six Beaver Dam students invited to the Religious Education teachers' homes one day weekly after school. Only a few of those kids came to the Sunday classes at St. Peter School. The program wasn't perfect, but it worked and it provided spiritual growth for a significant number of people, a number of whom weren't regular Mass attendees. Ironically, this model of religious education in a home with a person dedicated to children and moral values became the model for Anaconda as the Catholic schools' closure became eminent a few years later. Even in 2021, I am convinced this is still the best model for religious education for children. A structured curriculum is less important than a positive relationship between a caring adult and a child. Kids remember caring adults. They may or may not remember the rules of the Catholic Church. What will they remember in adulthood and why will they remember? Religious *knowledge* is always less important than a spiritual life modeled by a respected adult.

My term as principal in Anaconda ended in 1969 and I was asked to accept the principalship at Epiphany School in Chicago where I had been 1955-1959. (This was my first time in religious life that I was presented a choice, not really a choice, but a voice in the process.) I was not eager to accept that responsibility. I hated to leave Anaconda, but that wasn't an option. The Epiphany neighborhood had changed dramatically. In my initial service there, most families were Polish. In 1970, the school population was totally Hispanic and Black. School size was about the same but the principal did NOT have a classroom. White families had moved to suburbs or elsewhere. The neighborhood wasn't violent as far as I knew, but the school population was totally different and unfamiliar to me, again a whole new culture. There were fewer Sisters and more lay teachers. NOT having a classroom was not a situation that I would like. However, that task became my new assignment.

So, August 1970 found me (and my trunk) taking a train from Montana to Chicago and a return to a supposedly familiar environment. However in reality, it was much different to that experienced in the late 1950s. The friends made in 1950 now lived in the suburbs or elsewhere. In significant ways, it was scary and challenging, almost like learning a new language or way of life. The neighborhood was no longer stable. I never felt threatened, but caution was always a consideration.

The Sisters assigned to Epiphany that year were wonderful people and great teachers. The five lay teachers were also good workers and competent teachers. Most of them were in their classrooms at 6:30 or 7:00 a.m. preparing for the school day that started at 8:00 a.m.. Classes weren't as large as in the late 1950s, but they were large and all students were so needy. For Hispanics, language deficits were difficult for both teachers and students. Teachers were willing and did try different approaches to help kids learn. Epiphany still had no playground or gathering space.

As principal, I did have resources. The Archdiocesan Education people provided stimulating meetings and opportunities to meet other administrators. In addition, when appropriate seminars were available, I could attend. As a result, I learned many techniques about leading a school and about good teaching and learning. I always felt sorry for the daily burdens of the teachers, maybe more than they did themselves. It was a tough learning environment. It often felt like I as principal was an unnecessary appendage to daily life in a school. There were administrative tasks of course, but never as demanding as a classroom.

We Sisters had fun. Marge Conroy was a native Chicagoan and she had numerous connections, including the Sister-Administrator of Mercy Hospital. Together, they arranged evenings in which we brought food and enjoyed the evening on the roof of Mercy Hospital. Those evenings were delightful. Several Sisters knew priests who welcomed the opportunity to celebrate Mass at our convent. The local pastor/assistants did not choose to say Mass for the Sisters. Usually, with the guest celebrants, we would have dinner and significant conversation after Mass.

Several of my Sister friends from our preparatory years were teaching in Chicago Schools. The Dominicans taught at multiple schools in Chicago and the Chicago suburbs. My crowd and I were able to spend a day together occasionally at Epiphany. One of our classmates had been killed in a car accident, and once we shared a service in her memory. These were memorable occasions, always enriching and inspiring.

We Sisters had opportunities to enjoy the Brookfield Zoo and several museums and parks. Occasionally, we saw a stage play. Sisters had started driving several years before. Epiphany Parish provided a car for the Sisters' use and we had several drivers. I learned to navigate Interstate traffic and actually drove much of the city with confidence.

One time we arranged for all the kids to attend a *Star Wars* movie in a downtown theater. To our amazement, many of the students, even eighth graders, had never been in downtown Chicago. Everyone took city busses. We could board two blocks from the school and it was a one-hour ride. It was exciting for both the students and the teachers.

Two other Sisters were from Minneapolis. We established a connection to car dealers who needed cars driven to Minneapolis. We had to pick up the vehicle; the dealer paid for gas, and we drove, and delivered the car to a Minneapolis dealership. We spent the weekend with family and took a train from Minneapolis to Chicago on Sunday night, arriving in Chicago in the morning, taking a city bus to our convent, and teaching school by 8 a.m.. Crazy, yes. Possible? We proved it two or three times. One Sister was Alice Casey whose mother and sisters lived in Minneapolis. Alice and I were good friends. In the early 70s when I was back in Anaconda, Alice came to Anaconda and taught second grade at St. Joseph School. She too loved Anaconda. We still keep in touch. She's been married for years and she and Cal

Broughton have three adult children and four grandchildren; both Cal and Alice are retired. They live in Osage, Minnesota, where Cal grew up. Cal too was a teacher and Alice was a superb teacher and a wonderful friend always.

1970-71 was a good year living with good people and I know we challenged each other to do a good job in a difficult school environment, survived a changing time for Religious Sisters, and at a time historically that was confusing and constantly changing in the Catholic Church and in society. I enjoyed the experience more than I anticipated.

Spring 1971, each Dominican Sister was invited to participate in the decision about her assignment during the 1971-72 school year. The Sister who taught Social Studies at Anaconda Central chose to move elsewhere. With my BA degree in history, I was qualified for the position. At the same time, the push in Anaconda was to develop a city-wide religious education program for all Catholic children enrolled in public schools. This was seen as a response to a community need as envisioned by Vatican II and also as a preparation for the inevitable end to Catholic schools in Anaconda. I loved the idea of returning to Anaconda. The Anaconda Central principal, Father Bill Stanaway invited me to fill their vacant position to teach Freshmen Social Studies and Sophomore and Junior theology classes, as well as working to establish a city-wide religious education program.

That summer, the Mound offered a several-week workshop on teaching and administering religious education programs. Timing was perfect. Resources would be identified to pursue renewal of religious education programs. Father Cortese became interested, as it appeared that the task for Anaconda children would be our joint responsibility. He was given the time to attend the Mound workshop and we spent considerable time planning a program that we hoped would work in Anaconda in the near future. We both knew the resources available in Anaconda and we knew people who would likely want to be involved or could be coaxed into involvement. It was clearly a big task and needed involvement of many people for the program to get started and to improve with time.

That fall I lived with the Sisters who taught at Anaconda Central in a convent about a block from the high school. Both convents and the high school were on Third Street, several city blocks apart. Teaching high school students was a new experience and had its own opportunities and challenges. Shortly after the school year opened, one of the teaching Sisters at the school died. She had been ill but died suddenly. Experiencing a faculty member's death was a challenge for each faculty member and the students. She had taught there several years and was well liked by students and the community, A memorial was held in the school gym. Her body then was shipped to the Mound for a funeral and burial there. Father Bill Stanaway, the principal, accompanied her remains to the Mound. All deceased Sisters were and are buried at the Mound cemetery.

Keeping three Catholic elementary schools and a Catholic high school in a city with a population of about 8000 people was becoming financially more and more difficult. Pastors were pressured to provide finances in many directions. A decision was made to conduct a financial drive, hopefully to attract money from donors far and wide. Father Cortese was the responsible leader. He gave it his best but few donors were found. His health really suffered with the high degree of constant stress. He soon realized he'd been drinking too much alcohol, as well as smoking heavily. Ultimately, he took a leave of absence in September 1972 and was laicized in March 1973. Jim began to do physical work at the mine-waste dumps in Butte and later at a sawmill near Missoula. Eventually, and after we married, he worked for the Westinghouse Corporation in electrical sales (generators etc.) for about twenty years before retirement.

As Alice Casey came to Anaconda my second year, I returned to St. Peter Convent. A lady friend went to daily Mass. She picked me up; we went to Mass at St. Paul Church and she dropped me off at the high school. Alice had a similar arrangement with a St. Joseph School teacher who lived close to St. Peters.

Also that fall, I began spending alternate weekends staying with a woman who had multiple sclerosis and needed help especially at night. She lived with her husband in Butte. One of the high school teachers went to Butte each weekend, so I rode with her on Fridays after school and again on Sunday afternoon back to Anaconda. I fixed meals and slept in Ruth's bedroom each night. She sat in her wheel chair all day in the kitchen next to the stove; she often needed extra heat. She usually had to make a bathroom trip twice a night and I helped her. Ruth was a kind and gentle woman and we became friends. Occasionally, she wanted to go for a ride. I could get her in her car and we would go wherever she wanted. Sometimes, we would eat at a restaurant. She let me use her car on Sunday mornings so I could attend Mass and I became a member of St. Joseph Parish in Butte.

As it became evident that the Catholic schools would close in June 1973, plans were unfolding about what would happen to the students, teachers, the buildings and furnishings, as well as school records and significant documents. The high school convent would definitely not be used again for a number of Sisters. Sister Gilmary, a counselor at the high school, chose to stay in Anaconda and live at St. Peter's. She was an Anaconda native. Sister Gilmary had become involved with teen-agers who needed to move to more desirable, structured living situations and was instrumental in starting a group home for troubled teens. She continued with that ministry and also became involved with starting a food bank for the needy. Her mother was still living and she lived close to the convent. Anaconda Central High School was sold to the School District and soon used as a Junior High School. The lay teachers were hired by the Anaconda School District.

The summers of 1972 and 1973, I taught summer school in one of the Anaconda Public Schools. The second year, Alice Casey taught with me at the same school. For a number of reasons, each of us had decided to be dispensed from our vows and return to lay life. Alice accepted a teaching position in South St. Paul.

A Dominican classmate of mine, Marge Logan, later Marge O'Leary, originally from Anaconda, had left the Congregation several years earlier. Her mother and an aunt needed her care, as well as additional income. Marge had been employed as the Education Director at the Montana psychiatric hospital at Warm Springs, located a few miles west of Anaconda. She liked her work, but she needed additional income. When a public school teaching job became available, she wanted to make a change.

During that summer, friends hosted a bridal shower for both Marge and me. It was such a happy occasion. Marge married Emmett O'Leary that summer. Emmett was a widower with four children, including a pre-teenage daughter. Together, they later had a son and the O'Learys were a beautiful family. Emmett was the brother of our forever-friend, Anna Rose Shea. Anna Rose and her husband Bill were so kind and generous to all the Sisters. Their daughter Francie had entered the Dominicans right after I had arrived in Anaconda. Emmett died several years ago and Marge continues to live in Bozeman with one of Emmett's sons.

When Marge realized that I would be seeking employment in the area, she invited me to the hospital to meet her boss, Lou Wurl, and discuss the possibility of my taking over the position of Education Director. It worked out so well: Marge left on a Friday and I started the following Monday. Mr. Wurl was a wonderful boss. He'd been Director of all activity therapies for years, knew many of the patients and nearly all the medical staff.

In the school, three teachers and an aide set up individualized instruction for all school-age children in the hospital. Those numbers changed frequently as kids either got sicker and couldn't attend, or they got better and left the hospital. School-aged children were the first priority. In addition, if medical staff or others felt that being in a structured learning program would benefit the mental health of a patient, that person would be referred to us. I did the evaluations and assisted setting up the individualized program of study for a basic education program that could be designed in a variety of ways. For example, a business program such as bookkeeping and/or typing or related skills could lead to employment. A living skills program was taught in a classroom set up as a kitchen, so it included cooking or homemaking skills. All programs were flexible and suited to the needs of the client. It was a good program with caring staff. It was satisfying when people got better and left the hospital. More often, folks became long-term clients and the school staff helped to make their hospitalization less burdensome. Often, being a student increased their self-esteem and the experience truly served as a therapy.

The Department staff included recreation, music, dance, and occupational therapies. Other than the "school," therapies were conducted in other parts of the hospital. Recreation therapy, essentially any activity involving bodily movement, was sometimes conducted on patient wards.

That environment too was changing. Legislation had been passed that mentally or emotionally disturbed individuals who needed hospitalization should receive their care "in the least restrictive environment." In some cases, hospitalization in a state hospital was NOT the least restrictive environment. However, few communities had group homes and/or day treatment programs for mentally or emotionally disturbed individuals living independently. Political pressure was on administrators at state hospitals. As a consequence, people were often placed outside the hospital even when community resources were limited. As a result, the number of patients in the State hospital decreased and therapies such as ours decreased in numbers as well. Controversy continued for years about the decision to dismiss so many people from the State Hospital.

And, major changes occurred in my life. Jim Cortese and I married in November 1974. He was then employed at the Port of Montana, a shipping facility, just west of Butte and I was employed at Warm Springs. We chose to be married on Thanksgiving day, as that holiday represented our gratitude for each other and loving family and friends with whom to celebrate. That summer we met with Bishop Hunthausen who blessed our plans and continued to be a cherished friend until his death a few years ago. That visit provided a closure for Jim and for me as well. My dispensation letter was abrupt and included a check for under $100. Years later however the Motherhouse administration arranged several weekends for former Sisters to gather which were blessed events and far more welcoming than the letter referenced above. Jim attended two or three of those weekends with me and learned to feel comfortable and welcomed at the Mound with many of the Sisters. It was a special time to socialize with old friends and to make new friends as well.

Prior to our marriage, Jim and I had been regularly attending St. Joseph Church in Butte. The pastor was Father Ed Stupca, and both Fathers Bill Stanaway and Robert Shea were lifelong friends of Jim and good friends of mine. All had some association with St. Joseph's. We chose the wedding to take place at Mass at St. Joseph's at 1:00 p.m. on Thanksgiving day. We didn't prepare invitations but included a "you all come" announcement in the church bulletin. Some parishioners, many Anaconda friends, and at least twelve priests came to the marriage ceremony. When it became clear that a number of Gillens: Mom, Ambrose, Ruth, Greg, Varian, Rita, Luella, Ann and Alexius, Ed, and Adrian would come to Montana for this memorable event, we decided that a Thanksgiving dinner for family and close friends would be appropriate. Mitzi and Jim Daily, good friends forever, arranged with a friend Nancy McLaughlin to prepare and serve a turkey dinner with all the trimmings for about fifty people on Thanksgiving afternoon. Jim's parents, two sisters, one husband, one child and a few other good friends were invited to dinner in the parish hall at St. Joseph's. It happened without a hitch! All was lovely, simple and joyful.

Jim and I purchased our home on Grand Avenue a few weeks prior to the wedding and I lived there after the purchase. We decided to wait to purchase furniture until later. For all the wedding guests, we borrowed beds: two in the front room facing the street, two more in the extra bedroom and two in the third bedroom. Jim's parents purchased a bedroom set for us, and that was ready in "our" bedroom. And, good friend, Mary Keane planned to be traveling and offered us her home for wedding guests which we accepted.

Several family members stayed at Mary Keane's home, and the other out-of-town guests stayed at our home.

Ambrose, Ruth, Rita and Luella drove to Butte and arrived the day before the wedding. They were helpful with the final preparations.

We borrowed a couple eight-foot tables and some chairs from the parish. That provided space for eating and for playing cards and the Gillens were happy! The day before the wedding, southwestern Montana had a terrific snow storm. The Butte airport closed early in the day. The Gillen family members that were flying the day prior to the wedding had to land in Helena and be bussed to Butte. It was Mom's first airplane flight, and she coped remarkably well! Jim's parents had arranged for dinner at Lydia's Supper Club. Dinner was delayed waiting for the bus arrival, but it all happened and it was a lovely gathering of tired people, good food and few speeches.

Ann and Alexius, however, flew with a private pilot. Snow stopped them in Livingston the evening before the wedding, as it was not safe to travel to Butte. Thanksgiving day was beautiful in Butte. As we were leaving the house to go to the wedding, Ann called to announce that they had landed at the Butte airport. No visitors knew where the airport was so Jim and I took off for the airport fifteen minutes before the time of the wedding. Of course, Alex was eager to visit with personnel at the airport and acted like he had nowhere to go. I was angry with him and said, "Get in the car. We are late." They did. They went to the rectory to change and Jim and I walked down the aisle and into our new lives together.

The following day, the Gillens headed east. Jim and I had hoped to ski near Salt Lake City for a couple days. Snow was scarce, so we drove to Billings, enjoyed each other, returned home, and were back to work on Monday. During the next years, we drove to Billings several times to visit with the Dominicans there who included Sister Catherine Thomas and Sister Mary Marie, both classmates and good friends, and Sister Mary Bianca who became a cherished friend. When I was pregnant with Brian, we went to Billings to shop for maternity clothes, and yes, I modeled them for the Sisters! We also went with Brian and Jackie in their early years. I have a photo of Mary teaching Brian how to ride a tricycle on the massive front porch of the convent.

At Montana State Hospital, Lou Wurl was nearing retirement age and encouraged me to assume his role as director of all therapies. It was more responsibility than I wanted to assume. He and I talked about it several times. Finally I indicated that I wanted to continue in my present position. Some kind of a search happened. The person interviewed accepted and started employment. From the beginning, he seemed like a poor fit. He seldom interacted with staff and even less with patients. He didn't seem to choose to learn about either the employees or the therapies. Lou did retire and he and his wife Charlotte moved to Arizona. The new Department Chair continued as he did during his orientation and after a few months, he quit.

The next person hired was a man from Anaconda. He was more outgoing, but immediately seemed to favor male employees and quickly became a part of existing old boys' networks at the hospital. It was hard to figure out what he did with his time. He did not interact with therapies staff, other than the male recreation therapists with whom he played basketball. Morale that began slumping immediately after Lou left continued to decline. People needed to be recognized and appreciated for their efforts. Most staff worked hard. I felt that pain also and began to think about other avenues and opportunities.

Early in 1977 I learned of an Activities Director position at the Butte Park Royal Nursing Home on Nettie Street
and Continental Drive in Butte. I applied, was interviewed,
offered the position and started employment shortly thereafter. In the rush to secure other options for Warm Springs'
patients, a number of those people became residents at the
Butte Park Royal, so immediately, some faces were familiar. I was invited to hire an aide to assist with activities. I
knew friends of Louise Kuntz who indicated her interest.
As it happened, she was interested, was hired, and began
work shortly thereafter. Essentially, Louise and I built the
Department, as it had been without a Director or direction
for some time.

John Jette was the administrator. He had told Louise
that she would likely get a raise in pay after six months. It
didn't happen and when she asked about it, he said that it
would likely happen soon. It didn't. Several more months
passed and one day, he told her that he had an answer and
asked her to stop in his office. When she did so, he told
her that she was terminated. He didn't give a reason; she
assumed I had requested her termination.

When Louise approached me about the reason, I
knew nothing about any action. Immediately, I knew that
I was also being terminated. Yup, I was right. Before I went
to his office, I called Bill Kebe, Jim's brother-in-law who was
an attorney and asked his suggestion about my options. He
was as shocked as I was. Even then, people had to be evalu-
ated and given a reason for termination. Bill said to ask for
a reason for the dismissal, not to say much else, and to let
him know the result.

I went to John's office. He wasn't there, but my final pay
check was on his desk. I waited; John came and essentially
handed me the check. He was in a relationship with the female Activities Director at a neighboring nursing home and

suddenly, it became clear he wanted to hire his lady friend. As reason for termination, John said that I had not consulted with his lady friend. I knew her; we had exchanged ideas. Their patient population was considerably different from ours and consequently, we approached activities differently. I had years more education and experience than she did. Louise and I packed up personal items and went home feeling sad and unappreciated.

The most vocal of those opposing our dismissals were the Legion of Mary ladies from St. Ann Parish who came weekly to visit residents and to lead the Rosary in the Activity Room. They were furious and spread their furor at the facility, the parish and around Butte. Maybe it was gossipy, but both Louise and I enjoyed their concern and their attempts to salvage our reputations. In reality, our reputations were intact and stayed that way. It was clear that the decision to fire us was unjust and handled in a totally non-professional, insulting way.

Bill Kebe followed up with a registered letter to the facility's owner who lived in Butte and owned both the Park Royal and the Crest, another Butte care facility. Bill said if anything negative was heard about me or my work, he would sue in my name. We heard nothing.

I heard from a few staff members who were supportive, including the Director of Nurses. She called me again in a couple weeks. Bill's letter alerted the owner who then checked on John's performance, found out that John had been mishandling funds, and John was terminated immediately. The owner did ask me if I wanted to return. My feelings were still hurt and I had no passion or interest in picking up the pieces. Also, I was being paid unemployment insurance for several more months.

As it turned out, I had to have a benign tumor in the abdomen removed. The tumor seemed to be a result of the two C-sections relatively close together. So I recovered, stayed home with the children and was happy. Mom, Rita and Lue visited that Fall and helped me recover from the surgery.

Virginia McGreevey was a former Benedictine Sister with a doctorate in gerontology and a full-time professor at Montana Tech. I knew her family and had invited her to talk to Louise, me, and other staff professionally at one time. When she heard of my termination, she encouraged me to visit with Dr. Roy Turley, the Academic Vice President at Montana Tech, about a part-time position teaching English Composition to college Freshman. Tech had a popular petroleum engineering program. On the global scene, this was a time of trouble and struggle in the Middle East. Oil prices were sky-high, so petroleum engineering was an inviting degree program for new students to pursue. Through planned and structured recruiting efforts, Tech enrollment was blossoming with new students, all of whom would be Freshmen!

Roy told me that it would be the Department Head's choice, but that he would recommend me to Dr. Jack Mc-Guire, the Department Head. I knew Jack's parents in Anaconda and I had taught his younger brother in eighth grade. In January, I was offered two positions in one day: one at Tech for the semester and the second as a full-time religion teacher at Butte Central Catholic High School for which I had not applied. The principal at Butte Central was a priest who had been Superintendent of Catholic Schools when I was at St. Peters and we knew each other well. In each case, a decision was needed the next day.

Brian and Jackie were babies and a part-time position was more desirable. Having been involved in two Catholic school closings already, I didn't find the offer inviting. I accepted the Tech offer. A couple days later, I met my English

Comp class of twenty-five males and one female for the first time. Both the students and I had to figure out how this was going to work. We both survived the semester. I learned a lot. I like to think they learned a lot. I was informed by Jack McGuire that if Tech needed me the following semester, he would call me.

Tech needed English teachers that Fall and I taught two Sections. I was learning the feel and strategies of being one of three women in professional positions at Tech. Eventually, a few more women were hired, but we women were always a noticeable minority among faculty. At Holiday socials, for example, Jim was asked several times, "And what do you teach?" Those conversations were always amusing and tended to be embarrassing for the inquirer attempting to start a conversation.

I became active in the Butte Branch of the American Association of University Women and continued membership for about twenty-five years. Initially, I attended the monthly meetings which included an informative program. I helped regularly organizing book donations, as the yearly book sale provided funds for special events or Branch projects. Used book stores, and certainly online book purchases, were not available, so the annual sale was anticipated by community members. Over the years, I served as Branch Vice-President, Branch President, and Montana President, all one-year terms. I attended both State and National Conventions several times and served on a national Board. I learned so much about leadership, issues affecting women's equality and professional growth. I also applied for and received grants from the Association, including one that provided some financial support when I worked on my Doctorate.

Early in my years at Tech, I was able to arrange a visit at the college for the then national President of AAUW, Mary

Grefe. Tech seldom, if ever, entertained a female speaker/ leader. I felt proud to speak up for women, even if the voice wasn't my own.

One national Convention was in Minneapolis. A friend, Bette Larsen, attended and we stayed in the Guest Room at Gideon Pond where Rita lived. Rita drove us to the Convention Center each morning and picked us up again at the end of the day. She was our guest at a dinner and we enjoyed being together those days.

The final years of my involvement, the local Branch was not attracting new members and long-time members were aging. With few new people and little diversity, members did not want a leadership position or to be involved with worthwhile efforts like "getting out the vote." Rather than be grumpy, I didn't renew my membership.

Early in both my AAUW and my Montana Tech experience, I assumed the leadership in Butte to hold Expanding your Horizons (EYH) yearly conferences for girls as young as fifth grade. EYH was promoted nationally by Mills College in California. The first conference in Montana was at Rocky Mountain College in Billings in 1982 and the second was held at Montana Tech in 1983. The focus of EYH was encouragement of girls' taking math and science courses in school and introducing girls to careers that traditionally had only been held by males. Conferences were always held on college campuses to promote the idea to girls to consider college as available and receptive to female students. When I approached Dr. Turley about having the Conference at Tech, he was pleased, supportive, and he assured me that Campus resources were available and the college would also provide financial support if needed. Roy saw the Conference as an opportunity to increase female enrollment at Tech, definitely highly desirable. I continued to promote and support the Conference for at least ten years, serving as

Chair three or four years. I had just learned computerized word processing in 1982 and it was priceless in doing the many details that that leadership task required. At the time, Tech had two computers available for faculty use and one huge and difficult printer.

In 1981 I was awarded a full-time faculty member position at Montana Tech. A Departmental professor, unfortunately, became so alcoholic that he could not continue. His disaster was my opportunity. I had been teaching one or two Sections of Comp for several semesters. I continued that pattern and started a new offering of Intermediate Writing. A senior level course in Technical Writing was a requirement in several Departments. Intermediate Writing became a required course in some Departments and an elective in others. Some engineering faculty recognized that one writing course as a college Freshman didn't prepare students well for a successful experience in Technical Writing or success in their careers.

In 1983, a new full-time, tenure-track position became available in the Department. I was encouraged to apply which I did. Ultimately, I was selected from a pool of dozens of candidates from across the country. Needless to say, I was proud and happy about that accomplishment. I was truly grateful to be selected from more qualified candidates, many of whom held PhD credentials. Shortly thereafter, I began to think seriously of pursuing a doctorate. In my heart, I felt that I owed that effort to Montana Tech because significant members of the faculty and the Administration placed their trust in my being successful.

Since our marriage November 28, 1974, numerous changes have happened as Jim and I grow together. We loved our home, gradually got furniture and furnishings. The property included a two-car garage on the alley, and a large backyard, a small front yard with a hedge along the street. Neighboring houses were close. Howie and Cathy Wing across the street had been acquaintances and soon become cherished friends. Shortly after we moved, Grand Avenue was torn up for several blocks and sidewalks were constructed on our side of the street. Grand Avenue only covered a couple miles, but it was a cross street east-to-west for Butte traffic. It connected to Continental Drive which had an Interstate Exit on the south and proceeded north to uptown Butte.

Our home was large enough to invite family and friends and that became the holiday norm. Jim still had as many as nine aunts and uncles living in Butte, several of whom had no children. At least once annually, we gathered that group and it was great fun especially hearing all the reminiscing. They all loved Jim and their appreciation of me was evident from the beginning. Holidays were spent with Jim's parents and his sisters Kay, Virginia, husband Bill and eventually two children, Christopher and Angela. Chris was a baby when we were married. Often, Pat Casey and her aunt, Elizabeth Dougherty joined us, and sometimes Sister Sue Klein and occasionally a priest friend or two.

On March 23, 1976, we welcomed Brian Charles Cortese at 9 lbs 7 ounces. The pregnancy was easy, labor was difficult, and a C-section was performed for us to welcome Brian. Baby and I had to be hospitalized for a week which I hated. We got through it and were so happy to be home. The nursery was ready and Brian adjusted well.

On October 31, 1977, we welcomed Jacqueline Joanne Cortese at 9 lbs. 4 ounces. My gynecologist insisted that this second baby be a planned C-section. The date was a Monday and I hoped to be home by Friday. That happened. The second pregnancy was uncomplicated. Jim and I learned quickly to cope with two babies. Difficult at times, but mostly pure joy and total amazement!

Many friends in Anaconda died, and wakes were faithfully attended, often with babies in tow. Anacondans observed our behavior. We often heard that "Father Cortese and Sister Joanne and their kids were in town."

As time went on, Brian and Jackie became best friends which fortunately has continued into adulthood. I kept a diary for them in 1981 ff.. They have copies so I won't repeat those stories here. They were sweet, "easy" children and we always did our best. Parenthood is largely a guessing game; many days require decisions and a parent tries to decide what makes sense and is in both the child's and the parents' best interests. We enjoyed parenthood and now grandparenthood and we continue to learn. Now in 2021, we have four teen-aged grandchildren in whom we take great pride. We recognize similarities to their parents in their behavior and choices.

Daily, we thank God for our family and friends, always amazed at the wonderful people our lives have touched. Each time a memory from the past comes forward, it helps us recall the surrounding people and events of that time. It adds joy to our lives. We have been blessed over and over. Each life event and nearly every day reminds us of that gift.

Back to 1983, Brian started second grade at Webster-Garfield and Jackie started kindergarten at McKinley School on West Park Street. They had a superb Day Care experience at the facility on Front Street; they had both started there part-time several years earlier. It was next to Webster-Garfield School. Day Care Aides walked the kids to their classrooms. For Jackie that year, the bus stopped at Day Care and returned her there at noon each day. Usually, I dropped them off at Day Care on my way to Tech. The Day Care staff and their teachers were competent and caring people. My schedule was flexible, and I was always able to attend events at Day Care and at school. Sometimes,

Jim could get away also. We both saw those occasions as important.

We continued to be active at St. Joseph Parish. Before I became full-time at Tech, I directed the religious education program for a few years. Fortunately, Sister Sharon Smith, SCL had been wanting to return to Butte, as her family lived in Butte. When we started searching for a Director, Sharon responded and she was eager to pursue a ministry in Butte.

A year or two later, I agreed to supervise a Parish Directory project – photos, updated addresses etc. We got it done with the usual hassles and failures to show up etc.. I still think Parish Directories help build community in a parish or organization.

Jim was involved and committed to St. Joseph Parish RCIA program for new Catholics for many years.

Eventually at Tech, I began to teach an Introduction to Education class, the only education offering at Tech. Many students spent two years at Tech and transferred to other colleges. Many of those were people who wanted to major in Education, so an introductory class fit nicely into their course choices. I enjoyed it and it likely contributed to my own teaching skills.

A couple semesters I taught an introductory journalism class. One of those classes consisted of all female students, a first in my career. It was really fun. We all learned a lot.

Early in my full-time position, I was convinced that Tech needed a writing lab where students could go for one-to-one work with their writing. When word processing became readily available, I was even more convinced that a lab with 20 or more computer stations would enhance the writing curriculum and would be valuable for student learning.

Greg Sheridan was the Development Director for a few years. He was approachable and I shared my thoughts with him. He didn't really care about the idea, but he was a money man and any money coming to the college from an outside source was a feather in his cap. He suggested that we try Fred Meyer (the Kroger Corporation) and that we ask for $200,000. He had a guideline. I followed the guideline and wrote a proposal. The finance person for the Montana Bureau of Mines and Geology was asked to put together a three-year budget proposal to accompany the paper. Essentially, the numbers were demonstrating the $200,000 expenditure for the computer lab with appropriate numbers, as well as money the College would spend for the purpose. My writing demonstrated why the Lab was needed, what it would include, and how students would benefit from the availability of the Lab. Greg helped me polish it and encouraged me to talk to the college President, Dr Fred DeMoney, about the proposal and the project.

That precipitated my first professional conversation with Fred DeMoney. Much to my surprise, he was extremely supportive of the idea and it was a productive visit. Fred Meyer did not fund my dream. However, my conversation motivated the college President to follow through on the idea and that Fall, Tech opened its first computer lab! No one was more surprised than I was. I taught a one-credit word processing class in the Lab that Fall and encouraged all my students to use the Lab and provided help when needed. Within a few weeks, the Lab was busy at all hours. Very soon, plans were underway from the Engineering faculty to create their own Lab. That was just the beginning of student use of computers on the Tech campus.

A few years later, two women who had been students of mine and graduated from Tech and employed in computer-intensive, cutting-edge work – one in the Silicon Valley and the other with Sun Systems in Colorado asked me if they could come to Tech to talk to faculty about the

Internet. No one at Tech had even heard of the Internet. Jim Michelotti chaired the Computer Science Department. He trusted me and listened to the idea and agreed that it was a good idea to have these women come to talk to faculty. Jim Michelotti made sure his technical workers attended and it was an intensive personal growth experience for all involved. Yvonne and Lynn were thrilled to come and share their expertise, young professionals that they were. The attendees were attentive and challenged, and ultimately, the Tech computer Labs (several by then) had Internet access. Again, no one was more amazed than I was.

Another exciting challenge was an invitation from Dr. Fred deMoney, who after retirement from Tech, pursued other avenues to enhance the college. He had contacts with the Freeport-McMoran Gold Mine in Irian Jaya, Indonesia. He had visited there and learned that Freeport was under pressure from the Indonesian Government to move more native men (all men, of course) into management positions. To do so required additional knowledge of mining engineering strategies and administrative skills. Fred proposed that several of the present Freeport employees come to Montana Tech. He assured mine management that an individualized program for each miner would be prepared; it would include class work at Montana Tech and on-the-job training at Montana Resources, the active mining group in Butte. Fred invited a retired miner and friend of the college, Joe Chelini, to direct the program. The proposal was accepted.

Fred contacted me and asked me to work with the Indonesians on their English skills and better comprehension of American culture. He offered me a contract to assure payment for my service.

I participated for three groups – four men, two men, three men – over a three-semester time frame. It was challenging and great fun. Each man had understandable and useable skills in English to build on. A house and a car were purchased for their use. My first task with the first group was to assist them to pass the written test to procure a Montana driver license. Each man drove in Indonesia, largely mine trucks of course. Driving on city streets or U.S. Interstates etc. was totally new. It was a challenge; they passed the exam!

Subsequent groups were younger men, and they seemed to adapt to American culture quickly. The third group was skilled enough in language skills to be incorporated into a Business and Professional Writing class that I taught. That also gave them additional opportunities to interact with American students, enhance their writing skills and class participation provided them a unique challenge of communicating with people from another culture. I loved the challenge and the experience. It was so beneficial to the American students, as few ever had the opportunity to interact comfortably with people thousands of miles from their comfort level. I still recall many funny experiences, as I wanted to make the most of this opportunity for students to experience diversity. I doubt that the American students had any idea of the cultural shock experienced by these visitors to the U.S.. They were all good people, like 99 percent of my thousands of students in nearly fifty years in a classroom.

To this day, I hear from a couple of the Indonesians occasionally. I don't know if any one became a manager. I hope so, but that goal was beyond my control. Both Joe Chelini and Fred deMoney died many years ago.

My other international experience stemmed from our many-years friendship with Father Steve Judd, a Maryknoll missioner, who grew up in Butte with his parents and brothers. His parents owned and operated the New Deal Bar all their lives and raised their four sons in the apartment above the bar. Several years after becoming a priest, Steve wrote an article for the *Maryknoll Magazine* called "Saloon Spirituality" a topic so familiar to him as he had listened to his parents counsel bar clients all during his childhood.

Steve now 74 spent more than one-half his life working with people in Peru and Bolivia trying to meet their spiritual needs.

When he visited Butte sometime in the 1990s, he was newly assigned as a college chaplain at the University of Puno in Peru. He would be the first resident chaplain at that University. He realized that he would need to visit with administrators, faculty, staff, and students to become familiar with their concerns/needs to understand his role as a priest in a public university. The University was located in the mountains near Lake Titicaca. Faculty members were beginning to do research about mine wastes including the harmful chemicals in Lake Titicaca.

We visited several times while Steve was in Butte. I was always looking for ways to help my college students have a better understanding and appreciation for people of other cultures. Steve and I exchanged ideas about how his students in Puno, Peru and my students in Butte might interact or at least become aware that college students universally had talents and similar experiences to share.

As Steve met administrators on the Puno campus, some were already aware of Montana Tech, particularly the research being done in environmental engineering in general and mine wastes specifically. Shortly thereafter, I received an impressive-looking, official document written in Spanish and from the University of Puno. I had done some work with the Dean of the Graduate School, Dr. Joe Figuera and he could read Spanish. He did read it and he told me that he would discuss the proposal from the University of Puno with the Chancellor of Montana Tech. Puno administrators were suggesting a reciprocal agreement with Montana Tech, apparently not too unusual between South American and North American academic institutions.

After only a few months, two Tech professors of environmental engineering spent several weeks at the University of Puno sharing concerns and significant research that benefitted students in both schools. Steve met them at the airport and arranged for their housing. The working relationship between both Universities that began with that initial faculty exchange continued and it may still be going on. The next time Steve came to the U.S., Tech hosted a reception to honor both of us! It always amazed me how a couple conversations in our home in Butte affected the lives of people internationally.

We visited with Steve recently. He is living in Butte and in the process of writing a book about the contribution of the Maryknoll Fathers and their co-workers in Latin America over many decades of service. Their lives are changing also, as their priests now number 200 men with an average age above seventy years. In the 1970s when Steve entered Maryknoll after several years in the United States Air Force, priest numbers exceeded 1200.

I have mentioned Dr. Turley several times. When he chose to retire as Academic Vice-President at Tech, he and his wife Shirley attended an Episcopal seminary in Wisconsin and he became an Episcopal priest. I felt truly honored when he asked me to write a letter of recommendation for him to attend seminary to pursue his dreams. After he was ordained, he invited us to attend his first Mass at St. John Episcopal Church in Butte. He spent his priesthood in service to the people of Ennis, Montana. He died some years ago; his wife Shirley lived into her mid-nineties in Butte until her death in 2021. Both were remarkably kind, admirable, and generous people who had come to Tech from a small college in Ohio, contributed in countless ways to Montana Tech and the Butte Community and went on to a continuation of lives of service in rural Montana. Their values spoke loudly.

I mentioned earlier a fleeting desire to pursue a Doctoral Degree. I researched possible programs that might be feasible. I was cautioned to avoid a source in which the applicant essentially bought a diploma, actually only a piece of paper. In that process, I became aware of fully accredited Nova University (later Nova Southeastern University) in Fort Lauderdale, Florida. Nova reached out to people like me with excellent experiences in a field of study who wanted to hold a Doctoral Degree that matched the day-to-day work/efforts of the applicant. Furthermore, the process was geared to remote learning with several seminars or workshops on or off campus over a three-year period. It clearly involved commitment and perseverance, but it was doable. I started in 1986 with an initial visit to Orlando, Florida for a week-long Education Conference, and a first meeting with Nova faculty and classmates beginning the program, and a course of study to begin immediately.

These were the early days of the Internet and word processing. We moved our family computer into the living room near the kitchen. Brian and Jackie were in Middle School and were quite independent, but I didn't want to be alone in a room for hours as I pursued my studies. Studies weren't earth-shaking and were sometimes boring, but I had a goal and steps to arrive at an EdD Degree in Computer Education. I was truly interested in the topic and the goal which I achieved with my Doctoral Degree in 1990. I did travel to Florida several times and once to Los Angeles for in-person seminars. The maraschino cherry on the accomplishment was a family trip to Florida to attend my

Commencement Service (boring!) and to visit Disneyworld and other Florida sites. We all enjoyed it. Actually, our family earned that award and that trip.

Subsequently, I was awarded a full Professorship at Montana Tech. That was another goal achieved. It increased my salary significantly as I began to consider retirement in the future.

Awards were fun! I received the Montana Professor of the Year Award, the first time for a Tech faculty member. Dr. Tom Waring, the Academic Dean then, initiated, encouraged and supported my application. I was the Tech Professor of the Year a couple times. The latter did not require an application and a financial award was attached. There were some other less significant awards, but fun too! The Montana Professor of the Year was announced at a Press Conference. About two dozen former students attended. They were as excited as I was and their support was so appreciated and no doubt, the reason I got the award. The final award presented to me by Montana Tech would be the Professor Emeritus title with a few perks and given to me at the final faculty meeting before I retired in 2001. It was a proud, emotional moment.

Sometime after finishing my Degree, an upheaval erupted in the Department. It was becoming clearer that more writing courses reaching out to a greater number of students were needed. The Department Chair and most of the faculty had been teaching at Tech for fifteen or more years and most of that group had no desire or willingness to change. Again, to my amazement, four of the younger faculty who were willing to change, proposed that the five of us would develop a new Degree offering. I was asked to be the Department Chair of this group. We made it happen! Shortly after the creation and enrollment into the Professional and Technical Communication Degree, we five endured the process of developing a Master's Degree in Professional and Technical Communication which required multiple meetings, documentation, and approvals at numerous levels of power, including the Board of Regents of the Montana University System. Again, we made it happen.

Ten or more students immediately applied for the Master's Degree the first year and two or three the second year. In 2000, the first group received their Degrees. All five of our Department attended that Commencement with pride and we each congratulated the recipients as they left the stage. Great students and great people. A truly proud moment for all.

The timing was perfect for me to seriously consider retirement. Jim had retired and we were both eager to enjoy our time together. Both children were in college and as it turned out, each was married a year after college graduation and had their own futures to pursue with little dependence on Jim and me.

Prior to the next semester, Paul van der Veur, a Departmental colleague, agreed to accept the Department Chair position. I indicated to the college administration and to Departmental colleagues that the 2000-2001 academic year would be my finale at Tech. The Department was progressing well. My retirement would allow hiring another faculty member with skills that I didn't have and the new hire would likely have skills that were needed with the two new Degrees. During that final year, I taught my usual classes, but stopped all college committee participation. I felt that Committee roles were to consider the future. I would be elsewhere and had no desire to plan for a future in which I would not participate or contribute to. I kept regular office hours for students. I did volunteer considerable time with the Montana Tech Foundation, assisting staff in finding grant-money opportunities. It was an easy year.

By the end of the academic year when I turned in my keys, the emotional attachments were already diminishing. I felt ready for the adventure called *retirement.*

During that year, Jim and I explored opportunities for volunteer challenges. After considerable research, we chose to volunteer in September 2001 in Chicago at a convent near Epiphany Parish where I had spent seven years of my life. An Adult Basic Education program was provided to the poor/needy in the area by two Dominican Sisters at the convent location called Connections. The Connections location at Central Park and Cermak Road was in the heart of the Black and Hispanic communities. Busses of Hispanics from south of the Border arrived daily in Chicago. Some were relatives or friends of these students. Students would report that three or four relatives came to live with them the previous day. Imagine, your family joined by several additional members with little or no warning of their arrival along with limited space.

In addition, six young lay people lived at Connections as Dominican Volunteers in a community setting and volunteered at other schools/services relatively close to the House of Connections. Jim and I were also invited to assist at another education program for teen-agers and for Hispanic adults learning English led by extremely competent Sister Ginger Phillips. We helped there twice a week, at Connections three times a week in the morning and every evening Monday-Friday. Sister Marilyn Derr tirelessly and generously led that program. She served so many people in so many ways.

Jim and I had driven to Chicago (along with a Tech contribution of several computers!), so we had a vehicle at our disposal. It was parked on the street; we had no problems with our own safety or that of our Buick. Immediate neighbors were very watchful of the Sisters, the other volunteers, and their vehicles.

The Chicago Transit Authority elevated train, the "El", had a station one city-block from Connections. Most afternoons, Jim and I explored the city. We learned the days with free admission for Seniors at the many Chicago museums, parks and attractions. We would figure out the El transportation to the site and the adventures were enjoyed. We could only endure crowds for a few hours and this arrangement was perfect for our amusement and education. Local culture was 180 degrees different from Montana. Gunshot sounds were common. Personal safety became a priority. Adults and young people with whom we worked were so needy. They were eager to share their stories, most of which were beyond the comprehension of white, Christian people like us.

A story we enjoyed was about a Sister who had lived at that convent. She kept several cans of vegetables on her window sill on the third floor. If a commotion occurred on the school playground below her window, she would drop cans of vegetables one at a time until the crowd disbursed. Did you know cans of vegetables could serve as weapons? Amazing new information…

Almost every weekend, Sister Ginger arranged for some event that she thought we would enjoy. All adventures were wonderful. One Sunday we went to Mass at St. Sabina Church, a Black Parish with an outstanding pastor, Father Michael Pfleger, who is still known in much of Chicago for his advocacy for the Black community. Mass lasted several hours, as music and dancing were an integral part of the liturgy. We loved the collection routine. As people entered, each was given an envelope. At collection time, everyone proceeded to the front waving that envelope – many wearing white gloves. They sang and danced to the front where people stood with baskets in which ALL deposited their envelopes with or without cash.

Another Sunday we attended Mass at Old St. Patrick's Church in downtown Chicago. Literally, thousands of people attend Mass there on Sundays. The church is filled and the overflow crowd attends Mass at the lower level via video. Often, the new worshippers overlap with the folks from the previous Mass. Several police officers direct traffic. The liturgy is prayerful and the homily, prepared.

Other times we had dinner at restaurants of a specific culture, e.g. Greek or Italian.

We travelled to Boston for a few days shortly after the 9/11 tragedy. Airport travel that trip was unlike any other. Armed officers were everywhere at O'Hare in Chicago. The Detroit Airport was like a funeral home as amazingly few people were on the move. No additional security was visible in Boston. However, Hanscom Air Force Base was on high alert. Jim and I had to be carefully questioned, although Brian and Becky lived on the Base. We visited them there a couple times and one time, we met them in New York City. Big city driving always appeared to be easy for them which added monumentally to our visiting many historical sites.

A moving and memorable experience was enjoyed on a Sunday following 9/11/2001. Sixteen high school choirs and the Chicago Symphony Orchestra performed together at the Chicago Symphony Center as a memorial tribute to victims of the tragedy. It was unbelievably beautiful. Every seat seemed to be embraced by beautiful music from all sides. Being in Chicago and being away from home on 9/11 has frightening memories, the exact opposite of the concert. The day prior to the concert, Jim and I went to Brookfield Zoo; entrance was free and people were welcomed to a quiet place outdoors. Plus, a tented butterfly exhibit was on loan. The day was a beautiful contrast to the events of that previous, mind-numbing week.

We spent two months at Connections. As planned, we attended a Call to Action Conference held at a hotel near O'Hare Airport the weekend before we left Chicago. We laughed at ourselves about the following experience. We had decided to spend the night previous to the conference at a nice hotel in the suburbs. During the night there we heard gunshots and general commotion. (Where are canned vegetables when needed during the night?) When we looked out the window, sure enough, we saw a number of policemen and people in handcuffs. Thankfully, whatever happened happened in another building and we were perfectly safe, as we had been all the noisy nights of the previous two months.

In 2004 we joined a tour group of seventeen travelers on an inspiring, spiritually renewing trip to Ireland called "Illuminated Journey." Although we visited many of the traditional tourist sites, the tour Director emphasized the spiritual connections to the sites whenever it was appropriate. Dursey Island off the southwestern coast from which Catherine Cortese's parents emigrated was not part of the tour, nor was much of County Cork from which many Butte people emigrated. However, we had several moving Atlantic Ocean experiences highly likely similar to those of Cork, Dursey, and Calf Rock – the latter the site of the daring rescue of six stranded Lighthouse workers by Jim's great grandfather, Captain Michael O'Shea in 1881.

We made a couple trips to Phoenix. Luella's daughter Elaine Johnston and her husband and family lived in Phoenix much of Elaine's married life. Luella visited many times. Twice, Rita joined her on the trip. Both times, Jim and I drove to Phoenix to enjoy visits with them and with Elaine and family, as well as other friends in the area. Of course, we took citrus fruit home to Montana.

Las Vegas was another destination for several trips, the most significant of which was the birth of Ella Marie Cortese on May 3, 2006. She was born at the Nellis Air Force Base Hospital and back home with her Mom the next day. Nate was so busy about his life that he didn't seem to notice her much initially.

Twice, eight Gillen nieces bowled in a National Tournament in Las Vegas. Jim and I were their official cheerleaders. It also gave us the opportunity to visit a forever friend, Gene Sajcich. Gene grew up in Anaconda, was a priest in the Helena Diocese, and was the Chaplain at Warm Springs State Hospital when I was employed there.

Brian's and Jackie's college graduations in and near Portland, OR were the most emotionally exciting travels of all. Brian and Becky graduated the same year – Brian in electrical engineering and Becky in Nursing. That event was highlighted by their announcing their engagement to marry. In addition, Becky joined the Catholic Church at a memorable ceremony at the Chapel of Christ the Teacher on the University of Portland campus. After Graduation, Becky worked in Portland and Brian at the Air Force Base in Great Falls, Montana. A year later, they married in Ellensburg, Washington at St. Andrew's Church and then moved to Del Rio, TX where Brian started pilot training and Becky nursed at a local hospital.

Jackie graduated from Pacific University with a Master's degree in Physical Therapy and was the valedictorian of her class. She delivered a moving address to her classmates and faculty. The year she graduated, Pacific introduced a Doctoral degree in Physical Therapy. Jackie's class had already studied most of the material to be presented to the Doctoral students, so that year only, Pacific added one summer class and considered initial employment as an internship. Following completion of those requirements, Jackie and her classmates who chose to participate were then awarded a Doctoral Degree soon to be a requirement for practicing physical therapy. After Graduation, Jackie got a job in a hospital setting in Mandan, North Dakota. She and Marty Mrachek became friends in graduate school at Pacific. After completion of his Optometry studies, Marty accepted a position in Bismarck. They married each other in Mandan, North Dakota a year later and made their home in Bismarck. Soon after, Jackie got a job with MedCenter One (later Sanford Health) in Bismarck.

Colleen and Joe D'Arcy, friends from our early days in Anaconda, moved to the Portland area many years prior to these events. Both were repeatedly so thoughtful of Brian and Jackie during their college years. Ironically, the D'Arcy's son graduated from the University of Portland and their daughter from Pacific University some years prior to the Cortese time in Portland and Forest Grove. Actually, Colleen introduced Jackie to Pacific. The rest is history. Wonderful, generous friends of our family.

Some months after we left Chicago in October 2001 and were home in Butte, we were asked to consider assuming the role of co-Directors of the Butte Emergency Food Bank. We had each served terms on the Board of the Food Bank; Jim had assisted with the accounting for years and I chaired the Board for several years. Howie Wing started us and our children as helpers on city-wide Food Drives twice annually. Jim and I had volunteered as workers of various tasks. The more we thought about it, the more compelled we felt to accept the new role which we did early in 2002 and served in that role for nearly ten years.

At the very first Board meeting, Jim commented that for the ongoing service and future of the Food Bank, a more functional building was needed. (Neither of us remember his *planning* to make that comment.) People agreed. I doubt that anyone believed it would happen. Jim starting looking and talking with people. We met with Karen Byrne, a manager at Butte Silver-Bow in future planning with particular emphasis on the renewal of the East Side of Butte. She encouraged and also did monumental work on a federal grant proposal for funding. There was every reason to believe that the number of people in Butte who needed food assistance was going to continue and probably increase. Housing and employment needs followed a similar pattern which also indicated that food need was not going to go away.

A warehouse building at 1019 East Second Street had been vacant for years. The property was in the real estate hands of Shea Realty in Butte. Along with Board members, we looked at the building critically and it was immediately clear that it was a perfect building and location for the Butte Emergency Food Bank. The owner was Bearings Incorporated with offices in Ohio. Bearings had their own real estate Division and those offices were in Chicago. One can see quickly that this purchase could be seriously convoluted, and for awhile, it was. The asking price was $700,000.

Margie Thompson, whose family was a consistent financier of the Food Bank, strongly suggested that we talk to someone in management at Bearings. Doing some research on the Company at a page on their WEB site, readers were encouraged to contact the Company Board if he or she had concerns for Bearings. Moreover, a Board member would respond within 24 hours. The Food Bank DID have concerns for their company which I expressed to them as their empty building and our need of that space. In my mind I thought if I were a CEO and the Company had vacant property several thousand miles away that had not been purchased for years and was being approached by a prospective buyer, it would be in my Company's best interest to sell it asap.

Amazingly, the following day, Jim got a call from the Chicago realtor for Bearings. Although Gary and Jennifer Shea were miffed, because they also received a call more unpleasant than Jim's call, negotiation for Bearings' sale and our purchase began at a rapid pace. The Food Bank had some savings, the federal grant was approved, Bearings reduced the asking price, and the Board approved our consultation with a local Bank for a loan. The purchase went forward. Again, as I said previously, no one was more surprised than Jim and I. Marko Lucich chaired the Board. The day that we three signed the papers for purchase, we were all in tears.

We made plans to incorporate a walk-in refrigeration unit and a walk-in freezer unit and other minor adjustments to the building. Both refrigeration units were large enough to accommodate use of a fork lift to deposit large loads of food. The freezer was such a gift at Thanksgiving time when dozens of twenty-pound turkeys were purchased. Getting the meat in the freezer required only a skilled fork lift driver.

Several local handymen showed up and made adjustments, one of which was a stairway ("to heaven") for easy access to secure storage space. Actually, the building had two warehouse spaces. At that time, only one space was immediately needed to greatly improve the situation. Over time, needs changed and the additional space was put to use. Presently, every square inch of the building is in use. Moreover and to everyone's joy, the Food Bank was debt-free within two or three years after moving to 1019 E. Second Street. What a miracle!

Northwestern Energy had surplus furniture perfect for our needs. The telephone system was enhanced to serve clients' needs more efficiently and to reach the various parts of a large building. I continued to write grant proposals for various needs as they emerged, e.g an updated fork lift, a floor scale (a fork lift could put large items on it for weighing), a floor scrubber. These and similar items required less lifting and were more safe for multiple users who were often elderly. Gary and Jennifer Shea gifted with a beautiful, oval-shaped, wood table for the meeting room. Community businesses and individuals were generous and gracious. Local media provided excellent publicity. When the move to the new facility happened, volunteers came forward and food was distributed one day at the old facility and the next day at the new facility.

Another blessing/gift resulted from a grant proposal forwarded to Congress by the then Director of the Missoula Food Bank. Missoula Food Bank needed a refrigerated truck, as they had a productive program to recycle surplus food cooked by hospitals and restaurants, re-packaged, and made available to Food Bank clients. Food safety required that cooked food be transported in refrigeration. She was advised that her proposal would more likely succeed if she requested trucks not only for Missoula, but for five other major Montana community food banks. Her proposal succeeded. Jim and I drove to Missoula and drove home a new refrigerated truck for Food Bank needs. Immediately with the use of the refrigerated truck, surplus food from WalMart could be accepted. WalMart repeatedly insisted on refrigeration from the store to the Food Bank. Volunteers Ed Harrington and Lee Andersen made daily trips to WalMart. They flirted with the warehouse female supervisor and the Food Bank received hundreds of pounds of food. One day, Ed saw an employee taking dozens of eggs to the dumpster. Ed intervened. Eggs were loaded on the Food Bank truck instead of the dumpster. The following 4th of July, Jim and I drove the truck in the Butte Parade and listened to the cheers of the thousands of parade attendees. It seems that all Butte recognized generosity.

Some years later, the Butte Food Bank successfully installed a commercial kitchen modeled after the Missoula success. It was another attempt to improve the services already offered. The kitchen provided other options to expand Food Bank contributions to the community.

The Butte Emergency Food Bank succeeded and continued to succeed with countless volunteers who serve regularly, some every day and some once a week, and some as members of a working Board, still others waiting to be asked to assist with a project or do more for the Food Bank as needs change. It is a remarkable success story. As the Irish say, "Brilliant!"

Food Bank volunteers enjoyed getting together. Pot luck dinners became a regular feature a few times a year. Many incredible friendships developed between and among volunteers. As Directors, we cherished their presence in our lives. In 2010, Jim and I were selected as Grand Marshalls of the St. Patrick's Day Parade. What fun that was! Volunteers made sure we had the proper attire and even the use of a green vehicle, complete with driver Sue MacPherson. Volunteers hosted a retirement dinner for Jim and me, held at the Butte Civic Center to which all were invited. Our children and grandchildren came and Father Ed Stupca joined us at head table. Once again, the larger community showed appreciation for the work of all the good people who served the needy via the Food Bank. That organization also operated gratefully on the shoulders of its founders and early supporters: Howie Wing, Irene Weber, Bob and Joyce O'Bill, Bob Freeman, Sue James, Bessie and Dick Rule, Verne and Edna Brown, Tom Alexander, Marie O'Brien, Marilyn Maney, Marko Lucich, Bob Carlson and on and on. Great people ALL.

Jim and I left the Food Bank in 2010 and left the Directorship in the capable hands of Kathy Griffith. Kathy clearly understands the mission of the Food Bank and its challenges and faces its future with optimism and courage. That continuation was another blessing for us. Long-time volunteers continued and new faces joined the group.

The next major decision in our lives was leaving Butte. As our children have homes and families elsewhere and as we both were closing in on 80 years, it seemed appropriate that we make our home closer to one of our children. Both children had gone to college in Oregon; we traveled west often. Brian and Becky married in Ellensburg, Washington, Becky's childhood home. Her parents Ginny and Paul Sorenson had welcomed us repeatedly during the early years of their marriage, so we had familiarity with the area. We looked at homes in Ellensburg and soon realized that having a home conducive to old-age living is what we needed. Brian and Becky looked for building lots and immediately realized two lots were available on Manitoba Avenue, one block from Kittitas Valley Healthcare, a few blocks from the Catholic Church, and from the library and downtown Ellensburg.

Inquiries revealed the owner Fred Huber, whose Construction Company had done work on Brian and Becky's home. Sale was contingent on Fred's Company doing the building. We met with Fred and discussed preliminary plans, including a house with American Disability Act provisions installed throughout our new home. Procuring a building loan was no problem; we hired Fred to proceed. Essentially, Fred's son and another worker did the greater portion of the building. We met with Fred and his wife Linda who kept track of all expenditures two or three times. Work proceeded as promised. Our beloved home on Grand Avenue needed no updates and it was sold by Sheri Broudy shortly after we left Butte on April 1, 2011. The trucker who packed furniture and our possessions in Butte was also the driver that would bring our belongings to Ellensburg several days later. We arrived in our new home the same day as the moving van. The truck driver hired an Ellensburg man to help him unload his truck. The helper offered to return and pick up the emptied boxes. It was a great help to us unfamiliar with recycling in Ellensburg. One of the first things we did was hang our family photographs and familiar hangings. Very soon, we felt at home. Landscaping and outdoor cement work was in progress. The garage was ready. Jackie and family visited in early May and we were ready to welcome them "home."

Of course, we missed Butte, our friends and Jim's sister, her family, and their cousins in Butte, as well as long-time friends, acquaintances, and customs in Montana. On the other hand, we had chosen to make this significant change and enjoyed the adventures as they unfolded. I did a variety of volunteer stints in Ellensburg, some more satisfying than others. Eventually, we did Meals on Wheels together weekly for several years and felt it was worthwhile, satisfying service. We did some tasks at St. Andrew's Parish, the largest of which was chairing the kitchen/dining responsibilities twice for the Parish Octoberfest. Immediately prior to the Covid19 pandemic, we became involved with a program for Hispanic people learning enough English to pass the citizenship test. It appeared to be a perfect fit. Perhaps, those classes can resume in the near future and we would choose to be involved.

We meet Patricia Casey, our Anaconda friend since 1964, weekly. Pat has lived in Yakima for years. She was employed with the Yakima Schools as an elementary school counselor for many years prior to retirement. Pat has no family here, and the Sorensons always include us and Pat in family celebrations. Pat, Jim and I are nearly "root" friends after all these years of a loving friendship.

Brian set aside a garden plot in the farmyard for us and it's a source of satisfaction and a worthwhile hobby for both of us. We've learned a lot about gardening. The soil is rich and we have improved it. We enjoy watching growth and we enjoy sharing our produce. From March through October, we spend time at the farm nearly every day. I enjoy keeping weeds at a minimum in the farmyard. The windbreak north of their home is a gorgeous treasure of natural beauty, often with a gentle wind that speaks of God and Creation. I like to pick up the pine cones, sticks and small branches from the trees and have built a substantial berm next to Cooke Creek that surrounds their property on two sides. My energy level decreases a little each year. We adjust. Both of us will continue to do what we can. I have planted hollyhocks in several farmyard spots. The Gillen family farm always had hollyhocks; the tradition continues thousands of miles west.

Presently, in April 2021, the U.S. and Washington State in particular are beginning to recover from the Covid19 pandemic which has controlled people's actions and lives for more than one year. During the last year, we have been at home almost always. Brian did continue to visit us. We did not have family or friends visit and we did not visit them. Last summer, Jim, Ella and I did drive to our Montana cabin near Georgetown Lake for a week. Jackie and her family visited us there. Today, Easter Sunday, Brian and Becky hosted a family gathering of Becky's family, us, and Pat Casey – the first gathering like that since Christmas 2019. Each of us has been vaccinated now. Nate and Ella will be vaccinated soon. Jim and I will fly to Bismarck to visit Jackie and family the end of April 2021. Jackie offered to drive to Minnesota one weekend for brief visits with my siblings.

In the Gillen family of my generation, Adrian, Luella and I are the remaining family members. Luella, at 99 years in 2021, is facing health challenges head-on. She has both Hospice Care, caregivers at Medford Senior Living, and a loving family who respond to her every need. Adrian lives alone. His needs are continuously met by his caring family. In a phone conversation recently, he couldn't recall details of something we were talking about. He stopped and said, "I guess there is no one else to call." I replied, "It's you and me, kid!" That's a show-stopper realization and another reason to count our blessings.

Jim and I face the future with optimism, totally confident in the loving care of God Who responds to our needs large and small. We have enjoyed blessings and opportunities for nearly nine decades on earth, and have every reason to be confident that our future is in good Hands.

The unknown adventure continues. If you wish, stay tuned!